AF303108

The American Pope

Bringing Hope To A Nation Torn Apart

STB.

Bibliographic information of the German National Library:
The German National Library lists this publication in the German National Bibliography; detailed bibliographic data is available on the Internet at http://dnb.dnb.de.

Publisher: BoD · Books on Demand GmbH,
Überseering 33, 22297 Hamburg, bod@bod.de
Print: Libri Plureos GmbH,
Friedensallee 273, 22763 Hamburg

ISBN: 978-3-8192-9038-2

This book is dedicated to all those who believe

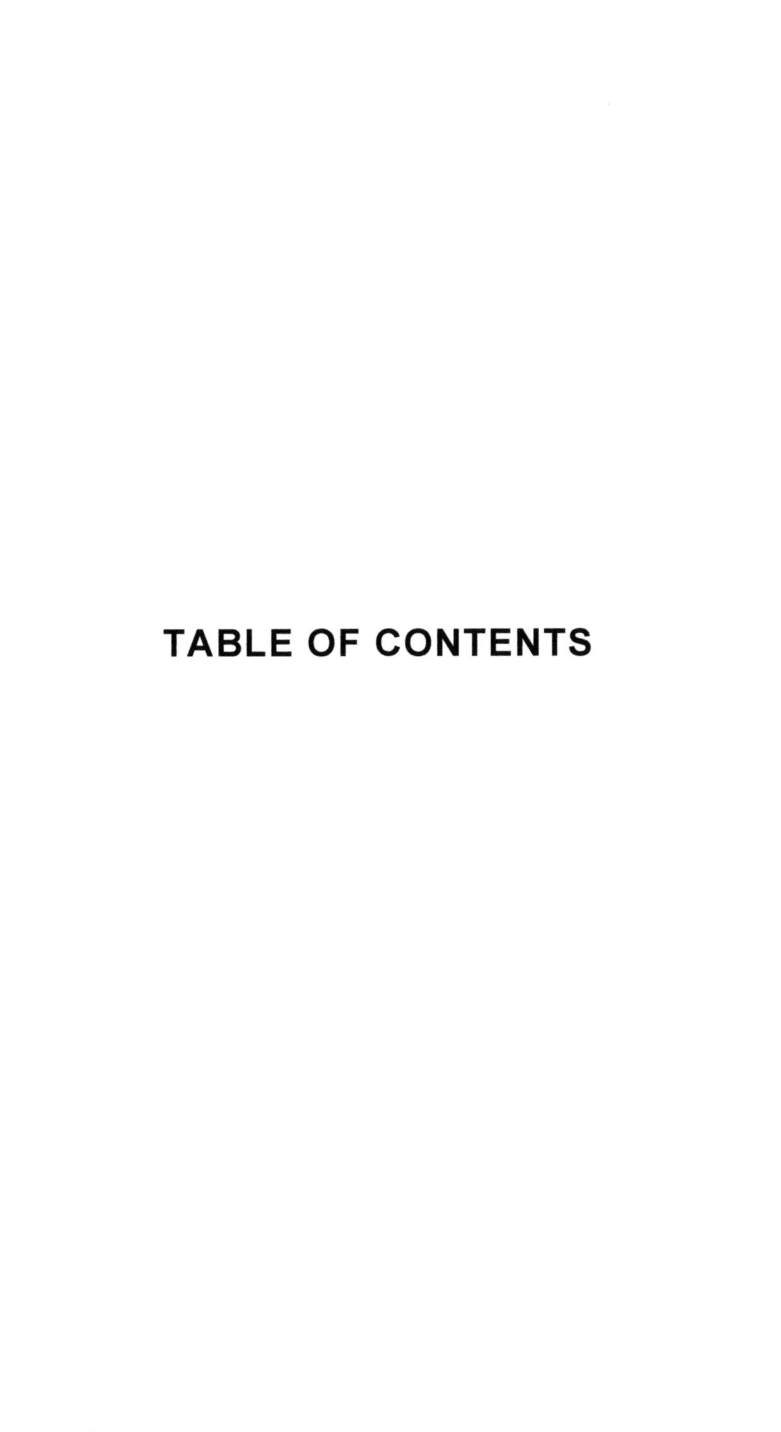

TABLE OF CONTENTS

INTRODUCTION

Pope Leo XIV was not elected into an easy world. When he assumed the pontificate, the Catholic Church was in a phase of institutional uncertainty, theological fragmentation and media polarization. While the secular West was increasingly struggling with a loss of faith and growing individualization, the Church in many regions of the global South remained on course for growth - and yet internally divided. It was in this field of tension that Leo XIV entered the world stage: neither as a revolutionary nor as a restorer, but as a man with a clear compass and quiet determination. At the same time, we are experiencing a geopolitical upheaval in which the United States - long a cultural and economic superpower - is increasingly confronted with inner turmoil, crises of confidence and a search for meaning. Here, in this field of tension between the loss of tradition, identity debates and the need for spiritual orientation, a pope is regaining relevance - not as a politician, but as a moral authority.

This book attempts to shed light on Leo XIV's role and impact in precisely this global context: Who is this man who so unexpectedly assumed leadership of the world's largest religious organization? What does he embody? And why could he be a beacon of hope for today's America in particular, providing impetus across denominational and ideological boundaries?

The study deliberately avoids ideological exaggeration. The focus is on the concrete actions, statements and inner profile of this pope - soberly analyzed, but with an eye for the essentials: the question of whether Leo XIV is a leader who can provide orientation in a time of general helplessness.

At first glance, it seems paradoxical: a religious leader who stands outside any democratic institution is supposed to have an influence on the political and cultural life of the United States? In a country whose constitution clearly regulates the separation of church and state, which upholds religious plurality and is becoming increasingly secularized? And yet the Pope's influence on America - regardless of the current incumbent - has grown historically and is structurally anchored.

Since the 20th century, the relationship between Rome and Washington has steadily deepened. Catholicism is no longer just the religion of Irish or Italian immigrants, but a significant social factor with over 70 million believers in the USA. Catholic universities, media and charitable organizations are part of public life, and Catholic voices shape central debates about life, family, justice and morality.

What's more: In an increasingly polarized political landscape, spiritual authorities appear more attractive again - especially if they do not make the mistake of taking sides themselves. A pope who acts not as an ideological actor, but as an ethical voice in a chaotic time, can achieve more than many MPs and commentators put together.

Leo XIV obviously understood this tension intuitively. In his first public statements, he repeatedly emphasized that his task was not to "govern states", but to "remind people". What does he remind people of? Of a different form of greatness - one that is not expressed in national power or economic dominance, but in compassion, clarity and responsibility.

This is precisely why this book is not primarily aimed at Catholic readers, but at anyone who wonders whether spiritual orientation - beyond party-political polemics - is still possible. In this interpretation, the Pope is not a religious monarch, but a cultural seismograph. And Leo XIV could prove to be the one who recalibrates America's moral coordinate system.

The election of Leo XIV was initially received with astonishment by many observers. Not a superstar of the medial church, not a charismatic reformer with an offensive agenda - but a reserved, intellectual-looking man whose name at first glance was reminiscent of monarchical times. And yet it was precisely this mixture of seriousness, theological depth and clever modesty that made him a candidate who did not polarize, but inspired confidence.
The term "bearer of hope" has become inflationary in political and religious contexts - often as a projection screen for collective longings. But in the case of Leo XIV, this attribution can be made more concrete. Not because he provides simple answers, but because he refuses to be taken in by the logic of exaggeration. His language is calm, his gestures

deliberate. And yet, precisely for this reason, he seems like a quiet counterweight to the shrill world of the attention economy.

It is striking that many younger people in particular - religiously searching but institutionally distanced - react to this Pope. They appreciate his way of taking ethical issues seriously without moralizing. They see his words on ecology, social inequality and spiritual emptiness not as a compulsory church program, but as a sincere attempt to enter into conversation with a disoriented present.

For the United States, where young generations in particular are increasingly critical of religion but open to questions of meaning, Leo XIV could therefore become a figure who builds bridges: between old and young, believers and skeptics, conservative morality and a progressive longing for justice. He is not a pop pope, but perhaps that is precisely why he is a credible bearer of hope.

America is a divided country. Politically, culturally, religiously. What was once seen as fruitful diversity now often appears as an unbridgeable front. The ideological divides no longer run only between parties, but right through families, communities and churches. Trust in institutions - be it government, media or church - is dwindling. In this fragile atmosphere, every voice that does not fit into the binary scheme of friend or foe is initially met with mistrust - and at the same time offers an opportunity.

Leo XIV approached this America with a mixture of distance and sympathy. He rarely speaks directly about American domestic politics, but his statements on issues of social justice, ecological responsibility, migration or human dignity have an immediate resonance - because they are ethically grounded but not charged with partisan politics. He names undesirable developments without condemning them, and he defends principles without using them as weapons against those who think differently.

Especially in the American public sphere, which often oscillates between religious pathos and secular cynicism, this form of moral clarity without moral arrogance acts as a counterpoint. It reminds us that orientation does not necessarily require loudness - and that the voice of reason can also appear in a religious guise.

Quite a few commentators have remarked that Leo XIV seems almost "American" in his administration - not in the cultural sense, but in his belief in personal responsibility, practical ethics and the possibility of renewal. He speaks of dignity, not power; of forgiveness, not punishment. And therein lies his potential to exert influence beyond the borders of the Catholic world.

For an America in search of an inner compass, Leo XIV is not a cure. But he is a point of reference. An anchor at a time when many are longing for something that will not disappear into the algorithm tomorrow. A pope who does not want to change America - but who can remind it of its spiritual depth.

Transatlantic values - Catholicism as a bridge?

When we talk about transatlantic relations, we usually think of military alliances, trade policy or diplomatic alliances. Far less attention is paid to an invisible but powerful bond: the cultural and intellectual exchange between Europe and America, shaped not least by religious traditions. Catholicism - once a European export, later a firmly anchored minority culture in the USA - is today a possible bridge between two societies that are both struggling with similar challenges: fragmentation, loss of meaning, crises of trust.

Leo XIV seems to have recognized this potential and consciously exploited it. Without lapsing into cultural-political lecturing, he emphasizes values that could unite both sides of the Atlantic: the dignity of the individual, the principle of responsibility, the role of the community beyond mere consensus. In a world that is increasingly characterized by economic rationality, his voice reminds us of a normative core that once supported both America and Europe socially - and which many miss today.

In doing so, he avoids simple classifications. When Leo XIV speaks of social justice, he is not pandering to left-wing milieus; when he stands up for unborn life, he is not adopting conservative rhetoric. Rather, he is looking for a synthesis - very much in the tradition of Catholic social teaching - for an ethos that combines economic reason with human care, individual freedom with communal responsibility.

This attitude makes him particularly interesting for American society because it opens up a rare space: a space in which moral principles can be discussed without immediately leading to ideological battles. In a culture in which "truth" often appears as a subjective good, Leo XIV offers a form of orientation that is not authoritarian, but also not arbitrary.

When America asks itself today what it wants to base itself on in the future, the answer is not just a political one. It is a question of values, of attitude, of dignity. Leo XIV does not offer a complete concept here - but an intellectual invitation.

At a time when public perception is often controlled more by algorithms than by arguments, the pontificate is also inevitably a media event. Every appearance, every word, every gesture of the Pope can be disseminated, commented on and interpreted globally in a matter of seconds. The question is therefore not whether a pope has a media impact, but how he consciously shapes it - and what the consequences are.

Leo XIV is not a media pop star, but he understands the mechanisms of modern communication - precisely because of his restraint. While many public figures rely on reach and polarization, he focuses on density and resonance. His messages are usually concise, well-considered and reduced to the essentials. Interviews are rare, but pointed. His encyclicals do without spectacular theses, but are effective due to their inner coherence. It is a strategy of minimal noise - but maximum seriousness.

In a world that is often defined by staging, it is precisely this non-staged presence that creates an impact. Leo XIV thus appears less as an actor on the political stage and more as a moral authority in the background. He turns against the dictatorship of the moment - and thus against one of the central mechanisms of the modern media world.

His global impact also results from the fact that he does not serve any specific interest group. While earlier popes specifically addressed internal reform groups or conservative wings, Leo XIV seems to primarily address the whole of global society. His words on the environmental crisis, migration and the economization of mankind resonate in Catholic and secular circles alike. In this sense, he is a pope of the space in between: between religion and the public, between dogma and dialog.

In the United States - a country with highly individualized media usage patterns and growing scepticism towards institutional authority - this form of communication seems almost countercultural. But therein lies its potential: Leo XIV does not force attention, he attracts it. And where others shout to be heard, he speaks - and is heard.

So what remains of this approach to Leo XIV - beyond the media headlines, beyond church politics and the current debate? Perhaps above all this: a gentle suggestion that orientation looks different today than it did in the past. No longer as an authoritarian voice from above, not as a promise of salvation through power, but as an invitation to think, listen and act.

In this respect, Leo XIV embodies a new form of spiritual authority. Not because he was revolutionary - but because he was consistent. Not because he was provocative - but because he challenged with his clarity. And last but not least, because he does not preach away the contradictions of our time, but names them - without claiming to resolve them definitively.

This book is an attempt to explain this authority - not to glorify it. It is not a hagiography, but an analysis. It is not a missionary work, but a political and spiritual classification. The central idea: in the midst of cultural discord, moral relativity and media overload, Leo XIV can be a compass - for believers and seekers alike, for conservatives and progressives, for Americans and Europeans.
So when the cover of this book contains the - deliberately provocative - claim that Leo XIV could "really make America great again", it is not referring to a political agenda. But rather a different understanding of greatness: greatness as a measure of attitude. Greatness as a willingness to renounce cynicism. Greatness as the courage to hope.
The following chapters will show how this Pope became who he is today, how he interprets his role - and why, especially in this historical constellation, he could have a global impact that reaches far beyond the boundaries of the Catholic Church.

And it will explain why it has to be an American pope of all people so that the world can be reunited - politically and in faith.

I - ROBERT FRANCIS PREVOST

Robert Francis Prevost was born on September 14, 1955 in Chicago, Illinois - a city that stands for the history of immigration and religious pluralism in the United States like no other. In the 1950s, Chicago was a place of profound contrasts: Industrialization and poverty, ethnic diversity and social tensions, conservative values and an emerging counterculture. In the midst of this mixture, the future Pope grew up in an environment that shaped him early on - culturally, spiritually, but also socially.
The Prevost family came from a typical US middle-class milieu with European roots. Catholic faith was not just a Sunday obligation, but part of everyday life. In this family, religion had less of a dogmatic character than a self-evident depth. Robert grew up in a household that combined education, prayer and community spirit. His parents were regarded as strict but loving - not fundamentalists, but people with principles and inner guidance.
Even at a young age, it became clear that this boy had a feeling for silence, for listening, for the subtext. He was not a loud leader in the playground, not a conformist follower - but an observer. A sensitive, alert mind that asked questions where others accepted. Why is there poverty? Why do people suffer even though they pray? What does it mean to do good when no one is watching?
These early years in Chicago were more than just a biographical backdrop. They trained Robert

Francis Prevost in the understanding of plurality, social reality and cultural tension. The city became a space of experience that shaped him deeply - not as a political figure, but as a human being. His later convictions - the importance of social justice, proximity to the margins of society, mistrust of dogmatism - are rooted in this childhood.

While many of his peers were oriented towards the cultural upheavals of the 1960s and 70s, Prevost remained grounded in a certain way: open to new things, but not naive. His Catholic identity was not reactionary, but reflective. And Chicago - with all its contradictions - was the ideal place for this: a school of life, diversity and responsibility.

Robert Francis Prevost attended Catholic schools in Chicago during his childhood - educational institutions that played a formative role in the social fabric of many Catholic communities in the 1960s. The school years were strict, but also supportive: in addition to a sound humanistic education, religious education was at the center. Catechesis, daily prayer and regular sacraments were part of everyday life. But what many children saw as merely a duty became an inner source for Robert.

Even at elementary school, he stood out for his unusual attention to spiritual matters. While other pupils memorized Bible stories, he asked questions about the meaning of vocation, grace and responsibility. His teachers - mainly religious women and deacons - later described him as "serious" and "atypically attentive", as a boy who not only understood religious symbols, but wanted to penetrate them.

The parish life of the Catholic community was not just a Sunday meeting place for him, but a social network that shaped him. He was involved as an altar boy, later as a youth helper and altar boy. But above all, he observed. How did priests talk to the poor? How did lay people behave in the liturgy? Where was faith mere form, and where was it lived conviction?

It was during this time, probably at the age of twelve or thirteen, that the first signs of a spiritual vocation began to appear in him - vaguely at first, later with increasing clarity. Not in the form of a sudden "call", as some saints' legends tell us, but as a slow inner certainty: that the Gospel could be more than a text, that the priesthood could not be a career path, but a way of life.

The proximity to the religious communities in Chicago, especially the Augustinians, was also a formative influence. Their combination of intellectual depth, pastoral service and spiritual community corresponded to what Robert was looking for: a church that thinks, serves and prays - in exactly that order.

In the Catholic landscape of the United States in the 1970s, there were a large number of religious communities open to young men who aspired to a spiritual life. For the young Robert Francis Prevost, however, it was not the big stage that appealed to him from the outset, but a way of life that combined silence with education, prayer with service, reflection with community. He found this mixture - with increasing inner clarity - in the Augustinians, the order that goes back to the church father Aurelius Augustinus.

The decision to join this order was less romantic than rational, but for this very reason it was deeply rooted. Prevost was intellectually gifted, but not vain. He was spiritually open, but not enthusiastic. And he was socially committed, but without missionary exuberance. The Augustinians, with their triad of community life, pastoral service and theological-philosophical depth, offered him a spiritual home that was neither worldly nor concerned with effect - but simply honest.

The spirituality of the Augustinian order, characterized by the search for inner truth, the combination of reason and faith and the radical focus on the love of God, corresponded exactly to the attitude that emerged early on in Prevost's thinking. Augustine's famous formula "Our heart is restless until it rests in you" became not just a theological quote for him, but a personal guiding principle. For him, it was not about external affiliation, but about a spiritual home.

In 1977, at the age of 22, Prevost officially joined the Augustinian order. It was the time after the Second Vatican Council - a period in which many religious orders were struggling with identity crises, recruitment problems and structural changes. But Prevost did not let this bother him. On the contrary: in this phase of uncertainty, he saw the need to rediscover the original spirit of the order - not nostalgically, but responsibly.

His entry into the order was not an escape from the world, but a step towards a deeper responsibility for the world. For the Augustinians taught him that those who truly seek God cannot avoid people. This ethos accompanied him from then on - through all stages of his life and up to the highest office in the Church.

After joining the Augustinian order, Robert Prevost began an academic career typical of many religious - but in his case it took on a special depth and direction. The order recognized his theological potential early on and sent him to study at one of the most renowned theological universities in the world: the Pontifical University of St. Thomas Aquinas in Rome, also known as the Angelicum.

Rome in the early 1980s was a center of ecclesiastical debate, structural upheaval and intellectual confrontation. The years of the Council had not long passed and Pope John Paul II was leading the church with a global church profile but a clear conservative style. For Prevost, studying in Rome was an encounter with the diversity of the Church - not only on an intellectual level, but also in personal exchanges with fellow students from all over the world.

His field of study was clear: canon law, later supplemented by theology. He completed a doctorate in canon law - a subject that many consider dry, but for Prevost it was a means of understanding the nature of the church not only spiritually, but structurally. He was convinced that order and grace do not contradict each other - they complement each other. His professors described him as disciplined, alert, modest - someone who did not want to shine through rhetoric, but through substance.

However, the spiritual atmosphere of Rome was even more important to him than the lectures. The daily Eucharistic celebrations in religious communities, the walks through the city of saints and councils, the personal encounters with pilgrims, cardinals, the poor and academics: all this shaped him into a person who knew the universality of the Church not as a theory, but lived it. The Church as a space between heaven and history - he became existentially aware of this here.

But Prevost never became a "church politician", even though he was later to assume the highest offices in the Curia. In Rome, he learned the diplomatic codes, Roman thinking and the intertwining of power - but he remained true to himself. Humility was not an attitude for him, but an inner corrective: against the temptation to vanity, against the power reflex, against losing himself in the apparatus.

His time in Rome not only prepared him for a career in the Church. It opened him up to what would later characterize his pontificate: clear but gentle thinking; a firm but listening voice; an attitude that never separated theology from practice.

After completing his studies in Rome, Robert Francis Prevost returned to the United States - equipped with a deep theological foundation, but without academic complacency. His concern was not the pulpit of the university, but the bridge between spiritual teaching and concrete life. During this phase - at the beginning of the 1980s - he began to put into practice what vocation meant to him at its core: faith that serves.

First, he made his solemn profession in the Augustinian order in 1981 - a step that sealed his final commitment to religious life. Shortly afterwards, on June 19, 1982, he was ordained a priest. The liturgical celebration took place in a modest chapel, not in a cathedral. For Prevost, however, this moment was not the beginning of a "career", but rather a confirmation of what had been in the making since his youth in Chicago: a way of life that was entirely dedicated to the Gospel and the community.

He spent his first years as a priest training and accompanying young religious. In the USA, he looked after novices and young students, taught canon law and spiritual theology, led retreats and pastoral talks. His style was calm, observant, never lecturing. Many of his students later reported that he "did not so much teach as inspire" - a man who did not lecture on theory, but conveyed a spiritual attitude.

At the same time, he was involved in social projects in his home region. At a time of a growing social divide - Ronald Reagan's America was characterized by economic restructuring, but also by the impoverishment of large sections of the population - Prevost became increasingly sensitive to the tension between ecclesiastical aspirations and social reality. His conversations with homeless people, immigrants, the sick and single mothers still shape his ideas of pastoral closeness today.

These years were not a phase of building a career in the church - they were a phase of inner anchoring. During this time, Prevost consciously decided against offers that could have led him into theological research or higher administration. Instead, he sought closeness to people, not to power structures. This attitude would later make him so credible in the eyes of many believers - especially in the global South.

When the call to Latin America came, he was therefore prepared - not strategically, but spiritually. What awaited him was a challenge beyond his comfort zone. However, Prevost did not see it as a threat, but as a continuation of what had always guided his life: the search for truth in the service of people.

Peru - An encounter with another church

The decision to go to Peru as a religious priest was a turning point for Robert Francis Prevost. Not only was he leaving his home country, but he was also consciously entering a completely different cultural, social and religious reality. The Augustinians had been running missions in Latin America for centuries - a tradition that was characterized by deep roots in the people, but also by a confrontation with the colonial past.

Peru in the late 1980s and early 1990s was a country in crisis. Economic instability, extreme poverty and political violence - particularly by the Maoist guerrilla organization "Sendero Luminoso" - put the social fabric to the test. It was precisely in this environment that Prevost began his service in the city of Trujillo, in the north of the country.

What he found there was a church that was not an institution, but lived everyday life: people who lived in the simplest of circumstances but prayed with deep trust; priests who were also social workers, teachers, therapists and pastors; congregations that developed an impressive spiritual depth despite material hardship.

Prevost did not do what many North American missionaries did at the time: He did not come as a "bringer of solutions", but as a learner. He learned Spanish with a regional accent, lived in humble circumstances, walked through poor neighborhoods and spoke to people without filters. He was particularly impressed by the unbroken faith of the people - a faith that was less dogmatic than existential, supported by images, songs, festivals and a deep sense of grace.

Prevost was quickly appreciated in Trujillo - not because of his background, but because of his attitude. He listened before he spoke; he acted without putting himself in the foreground. His closeness to the poor was not gestural, but authentic. He lived with them, not beside them. And it was precisely this that made him a credible pastor - for indigenous farmers as well as for young people in urban problem areas.

These years not only shaped his theology, but also his understanding of the church: not as a moral authority, but as "God's tent among the people", as he later put it. He learned that church presence does not consist of buildings, but of relationships - and that spiritual authority does not come from above, but grows from within.

His pastoral work in Peru was more than just a chapter in his biography. It was the lived response to his vocation - and the spiritual breeding ground for his later pontificate.

Prevost's work in Peru did not go unnoticed. Within the Order, he was increasingly perceived as someone who not only combined spiritual depth and cultural sensitivity, but also possessed clear leadership skills - but without a desire for power. His calm authority, his ability to provide guidance in complex situations and his modesty made him visible for higher tasks.

In 1999, Prevost was elected Prior General of the Augustinian Order - the highest office of his order worldwide. It was a choice made by his confreres not for tactical but for spiritual reasons. In this role, which he held for two terms (until 2007), he traveled the world, visited religious communities in over 50 countries, spoke with local bishops, helped resolve conflicts within the communities and represented the order in the Vatican. Here too, his signature style remained the same: listen, focus, strengthen - not dominate.

But his heart remained with the people of Peru. When the Pope appointed him Apostolic Administrator of the Chiclayo diocese - one of the most important dioceses on the Peruvian north coast - in 2014, it was more than just an administrative move. It was a return to his spiritual roots. Shortly afterwards, in 2015, he was officially appointed Bishop of Chiclayo. It was a decision that was met with great approval locally: The faithful already knew him, trusted him and saw him as "their own" shepherd - even though he was not Peruvian.

As bishop, Prevost was not an administrator in the cathedral, but continued to be the priest who went to the villages, spoke to fishermen, accompanied youth groups and was present both liturgically and pastorally. His sermons were clear, free of polemics, but with a high degree of spiritual seriousness. He spoke about responsibility, forgiveness and hope - not as theories, but as necessary practice in people's everyday lives.

At the same time, he campaigned for structural improvements in his diocese: for priestly training, for educational initiatives in poor regions, for intercultural pastoral care in a country with a strong indigenous heritage. He was a bridge builder - not just between cultures, but between the official church and the concrete needs of God's people.

These years in the episcopal ministry made him not only a spiritual leader, but also a pastor with an ecclesiastical and political mindset who knew how to combine administration and pastoral care. An ability that later made him so valuable for the Vatican and ultimately for the conclave of 2025.

In 2020 - in the midst of a global pandemic that put not only public life but also church structures to the test - Robert Francis Prevost was unexpectedly appointed to Rome by Pope Francis. Initially as a member of the Dicastery for Bishops, shortly afterwards as Prefect of this central authority, which coordinates the selection and appointment of bishops worldwide.

This function is one of the most influential offices in the Roman Curia - it plays a decisive role in determining who will lead the Church in the individual countries. The prefect must combine theological judgment, intercultural sensitivity, ecclesiastical political vision and spiritual discernment. It was precisely this combination that made Prevost the ideal candidate.

His experience from Latin America, his religious background, his proximity to the "margins" of the Church, but also his legal and theological expertise made him a candidate who was respected in both progressive and more traditional circles. Pope Francis particularly appreciated his ability to discern in depth - not superficially, not ideologically, but spiritually imbued.

In Rome, Prevost was thus responsible for the selection of bishops on all continents. Under his leadership, the work of the dicastery became more transparent, more participatory and focused on the spiritual quality of the candidates. Instead of focusing on church political affiliation or institutional loyalty, Prevost emphasized pastoral experience, credibility in everyday life and the ability for spiritual leadership.

Numerous appointments under his aegis - for example in Africa, Asia and North America - visibly bore his signature: pastoral people with spiritual depth, not careerists. These personnel decisions strengthened his international reputation - not only within the Curia, but also among the bishops' conferences worldwide.

At the same time, Prevost maintained his reserved manner in Rome. He avoided media appearances, gave only a few interviews and refrained from theatrical gestures. His office was simple, his conversations personal, his demeanor modest. Anyone who worked with him quickly sensed that power was not a goal for him, but a responsibility.

For Prevost, the years as Prefect of the Bishop's Dicastery were a kind of intermediate space - between the universal church and the Curia, between local pastoral care and global governance, between ministry and office. They prepared him - without him seeking it - for an even greater office: the Petrine ministry.

The 2025 Conclave - A Pope from America

On May 7, 2025, at 6:23 pm, the last clouds of smoke from the conclave left the chimney of the Sistine Chapel. Just a few minutes later, Cardinal Jean-Louis Taguem stepped onto the balcony of St. Peter's Basilica and spoke the famous words: ***"Annuntio vobis gaudium magnum: Habemus Papam." - "I announce to you a great joy: we have a pope."***

The choice fell on a man who many did not have on the list of so-called papabili - the "eligible cardinals" - until the very end: Cardinal Robert Francis Prevost, Prefect of the Dicastery for Bishops. A few moments later, he stepped onto the balcony himself - simple, calm, visibly moved - and spoke the name he had chosen: Leo XIV.

A historic moment!

This election marked the first time in church history that a US-American was elected Pope. The symbolism could not be overlooked: Of all people, a son of Chicago, a religious with experience in Latin America, one of the quiet architects of the Francis Curia, was now taking over Peter's legacy. For many, his election was seen as a signal of continuity amid change - a pope who would not imitate Francis, but would not turn back the clock either.

There had been much speculation in the run-up to the conclave: Would an African cardinal be elected? An Asian? A European for "stabilization"? The fact that Prevost was ultimately chosen was the result of a consensus on principles - not nationalities. He was considered to be spiritually sound, institutionally reliable and culturally flexible. For the cardinals from Africa and Latin America, he was a bridge-builder, for the European cardinals a calm reformer, for North American cardinals a spiritual realist without ideological baggage.

Although the exact proceedings of the conclave are subject to a vow of silence, it soon became clear that Prevost was seen as a candidate of the "third line": not as a progressive polarizer, not as a traditionalist counter-proposal - but as someone who was rooted in the margins and capable of dialogue in the center. Voices from the Vatican reported that there was a surprisingly clear majority in his favor - a sign of a silent but widespread consensus.

The fact that Prevost ultimately chose the name "Leo XIV" already indicated how he understood his pontificate - powerful, historically aware and with a touch of strategic symbolism. The last pope with this name, Leo XIII (1878-1903), was a social reformer and a mediator between the Church and modernity. A line that Leo XIV obviously consciously took up.

When Prevost appeared before the world public for the first time as Pope, everything about his appearance was subdued. No triumphal gestures, no emphatic shouts of joy. Instead, a simple greeting, a quiet blessing and the request: "Pray for me." These first few minutes sent a clear signal: humility before office. Service before honor. Responsibility before role.

And yet this moment was a historic turning point - not only for the Church, but also for America: the first Pope from the United States, elected not as a "representative of a country", but as a representative of a new type of spiritual leadership - quiet, with integrity, rooted in the global Church.

The choice of a pope's name is never just a personal preference - it is a message, a program statement, a hidden compass. When Cardinal Robert Francis Prevost announced the name Leo XIV on the evening of May 8, 2025, church historians and believers alike took notice. It was an unusual name for our time - powerful, ancient, almost monarchical in appearance. Yet precisely in this deliberate choice lay a theological and pastoral statement.

The burden and legacy of the "Leos"

The last pope with this name was Leo XIII (1878-1903) - an intellectual, bridge-builder and reformer. It was he who founded Catholic social teaching with his social encyclical Rerum Novarum and thus led the Church out of a purely hierarchical constriction and into a new relationship with the modern world. Leo XIII was a pope who appealed to workers, entrepreneurs, bishops and state leaders alike because he combined moral orientation with social reality.

Prevost - now Leo XIV - had referred to Leo XIII several times during his years as bishop in Peru and later as prefect in Rome. He admired the latter's ability to "interpret the signs of the times without submitting to them" - an attitude that shaped him as a pastor. His choice of name was therefore a deliberate link to an era of upheaval and openness, without breaking with tradition.

If we go back further, we find the famous Leo I ("the Great") from the 5th century, who was the first pope ever to be given this name affix. It was he who gave the papacy spiritual authority at a time when the Western Roman Empire was in decline - not through force, but through power of speech, theology and negotiating skills (for example in his legendary meeting with Attila, the king of the Huns). Here, too, there is a parallel to Leo XIV: the world is once again in upheaval, and the Church is looking for moral authority, not political power.

A name between strength and gentleness.

In the symbolism of church names, "Leo" (Latin: lion) stands not only for courage, but also for vigilance, protection and constancy. It is a name that does not bring with it any fashionable complaisance, but rather radiates seriousness, steadfastness and historical awareness. For a pope who seeks dialog with a fragmented world, but without relativism, this is a strong signal.

At the same time, it became clear that Prevost deliberately did not choose a "soft", spiritually vague name, as many might have expected. Instead, he opted for a name with backbone and reach - entirely in line with his own career: with integrity, unpretentious, deeply rooted.

Leo XIV is not a traditionalist in historical garb. His choice of name is not a turn backwards, but an indication of how tradition can be dealt with dynamically: as a source of clarity in times of confusion. The name "Leo" is therefore not a symbol of an ideological camp, but a symbol of a leadership style that relies on authority without autocracy - on attitude without harshness.

In a world that is looking for direction, the decision in favor of "Leo" is a message: the church will not hide - but it will not shout either. It will speak - emphatically, but without arrogance. And it will try to do what Leo I, Leo XIII and now Leo XIV have in common: Create hope where there is fear.

The election of Robert Prevost as Pope Leo XIV triggered a broad response worldwide - in church circles, political institutions and media commentaries. Within hours, the front pages were filled with headlines such as "A Pope from America", "A quiet reformer at the top" or "Leo XIV - the bridge builder between worlds". And yet it was not so much the sensation of his origins, but rather the tone of his first words that surprised many: sober, warm, unpretentious.
Within the Church: respect for style, hope for clarity
In the universal Church, the reaction was remarkably united. Cardinals from the global South praised his pastoral experience, especially in Latin America, where he was considered "one of their own". Numerous bishops' conferences from Africa and Asia welcomed his election as a signal for continuity in the global church - beyond the often Eurocentric structures.
Among many progressive voices, his election was accompanied by cautious hope. Although Prevost was not regarded as an activist or critic of the system, his decisions in Peru, his modesty in Rome and his willingness to reform as head of the dicastery indicated that he would continue rather than correct Francis' line - albeit in a calmer, more structured, perhaps more strategic way.
More conservative circles within the Church initially expressed restraint, but no open

resistance. Prevost was no stranger to them - he had never acted against them, never made a public front. The fact that he was a religious seemed to many like a guarantee of stability and discipline. No spectacular innovations were expected of him, but a spiritual clarity that had recently been lacking.

In the media: surprise, curiosity, projections.
The global press was mixed, but largely respectful. American media celebrated the election as "historic" - often with national pride and the question: "What does this mean for us?" The political discourse in the USA - often sharply polarized - reacted accordingly inconsistently: conservative media saw Leo XIV as a man of order and moral firmness, while liberal platforms pointed to his social ethics and closeness to the poor.

In Europe, his election was observed with curiosity. Some commentators in France and Germany warned of an "Americanized pontificate", while others saw it as an opportunity for a more global view of the Church. In Italy in particular - traditionally critical of papal elections "from outside" - he was described as "not Italian, but Roman in the best sense": someone who understands Rome, but is not captivated by Rome.

Political world: Diplomatic congratulations and quiet expectations
Heads of state and government around the globe sent their congratulations - from Joe Biden and Emmanuel Macron to South American presidents. Particularly striking was the swift and heartfelt comment from Peru, where Prevost was revered as a former bishop. The Peruvian government

symbolically declared him a "son of the country" and highlighted his services to the poor.

The Vatican State itself seemed well prepared for this election: Internally, Prevost was seen as a consensus-oriented man who could implement clear but non-confrontational reforms. Many members of the Curia breathed a sigh of relief - not because he was powerless, but because he was seen as trustworthy and predictable.

Conclusion: a pope who unites rather than divides The first major impact of Leo XIV was not the change in content - but the tone: objective, humane, unifying. At a time when many institutions were losing trust, he was elected to lead the Church as a figure who exuded credibility through his lifestyle - not through staging. And this is precisely what became apparent in all the reactions: the church had not chosen a star, but a pastor.

When Cardinal Robert Prevost became **Pope Leo XIV**, it marked a historic first: the elevation of a U.S.-born cleric to the Chair of Peter. In the United States, this unprecedented moment stirred a mix of pride, identity reflection, and geopolitical interpretation. The very idea of "an

American pope" touched something deep in the cultural imagination of a country shaped by religious freedom, immigrant Catholicism, and growing tensions between secularism and spirituality.

National Pride – With Caution

Across major U.S. media outlets, Leo XIV's election was widely hailed as a milestone. From Catholic diocesan newspapers to secular front pages like *The New York Times* and *The Wall Street Journal*, his biography was recounted with fascination: Chicago roots, Augustinian order, missionary in Peru, high Vatican office, then pope.

For many American Catholics, especially first- and second-generation immigrants, the election felt like a form of recognition – an affirmation that the American Church had matured from its marginal beginnings to global stature. Yet this pride was not without tension. Prevost himself had never presented himself as a nationalist figure. His ecclesiology was shaped more by Peruvian parishes than by U.S. political debates.

As a result, Leo XIV's election was embraced, but not appropriated. American bishops, including Cardinals from Boston, New York, and Los Angeles, expressed joy but emphasized his global mission. "He is from the United States," one noted, "but now he belongs to the world."

The American political spectrum, known for its habit of drawing faith into partisan battles, reacted in predictable but telling ways. Conservative voices praised his pro-life convictions and perceived moral clarity. Progressive commentators highlighted his Latin American solidarity, his focus on the poor, and his alignment with Pope Francis on climate and social justice.

But Leo XIV gave neither camp the satisfaction of easy classification. His first address made no political reference and spoke instead of "rebuilding trust, with mercy as foundation." The ambiguity was intentional – a reflection of a man shaped by service, not ideology.

Some far-right commentators criticized the fact that he had served under Pope Francis, fearing continuity with progressive Vatican policies. Others, on the far left, feared he would not press harder on issues like LGBTQ+ inclusion or church transparency. Leo XIV responded to none of them. His silence was part of his message: The papacy, for him, is not an echo chamber of domestic politics.

In Latin America, his Peruvian experience was front and center in media coverage. In Europe, attention focused on how an American pope would lead a historically European institution. In Africa and Asia, many saw in him a global South ally in Northern clothing – a man who knew life at the margins, despite a Western passport.

Even within the Vatican, there was relief that Leo XIV had deep intercultural experience and was fluent in Spanish and Italian. The fear of a "Trumpian" or culturally aggressive American pope dissolved quickly – replaced by measured optimism. His humility disarmed skeptics.

For the world, Leo XIV's election was not merely about geography. It was about a new papal model: not a diplomat, not a power broker, not a celebrity theologian – but a quiet man who lived the Church before he led it.

In the United States, the deeper challenge may yet lie ahead. As the first American pope, Leo XIV will be measured not just by what he says to the world – but by how he resists becoming America's pope, and remains, resolutely, the Church's.

Every new papacy begins not just with a name, but with a moment. For Pope Leo XIV, that moment came on May 8, 2025, when he stepped onto the central balcony of St. Peter's Basilica in Rome for the first time. What followed was not a spectacle, not a performance, but a study in quiet authority.

The first thing the world noticed was his stillness. As the crimson curtain was pulled back, Leo XIV stood without elaborate gestures, without the theatrics some modern observers might expect in a global media event. He did not raise his arms in victory, nor did he deliver pre-prepared soundbites. He simply looked into the vast crowd and waited.

The square was filled with pilgrims, press, and political observers. Many had never heard his name before. The cameras searched for signs: Was this man a conservative? A progressive? An American nationalist? A Vatican insider? Instead, they found a shepherd with the calm of a monk and the posture of a listener.

Words of Grounding

His first words, spoken with a firm but gentle cadence, were characteristic of everything he had done before:

"Dear brothers and sisters, thank you for waiting. Thank you for your prayers. Before I bless you, I ask you – please – to pray for me."

There was no doctrinal outline, no theological discourse, no mention of global politics. In a world that often associates leadership with noise, Leo XIV led with deference. By reversing the order – asking first for the people's blessing before offering his own – he invoked a model of servant leadership deeply rooted in Augustinian humility.

He then offered the traditional Urbi et Orbi blessing, his voice steady, his words precise, as if already aware of the immense symbolic weight of every gesture he made.

One of the most striking features of that first appearance was what he didn't do. He didn't smile theatrically, he didn't extend his arms for applause, and he didn't use the moment to set an agenda. Instead, he allowed the silence between his words to resonate – a quality more common to monastic liturgy than to political address.

Observers noted how his presence contrasted with many previous popes. He was not the philosopher-pope like Benedict XVI, nor the charismatic reformer like Francis. Instead, Leo XIV communicated by restraint. Where others might announce, he implied. Where others might clarify, he provoked contemplation.

Even his papal attire sent a subtle message. He wore the standard white cassock with no added ornamentation. No elaborately embroidered stole, no ornate gold cross. Only a simple wooden pectoral cross – the same one he had worn as a bishop in Peru.

When questioned later by Vatican journalists, a Curial official simply said:

"He didn't forget to put on something else. He chose not to."

What the world witnessed in that first appearance was not a dramatic overture, but a quiet threshold. Pope Leo XIV made clear from the beginning that his pontificate would not be built on ideological signaling or performative leadership. It would be measured instead by something slower, deeper: consistency, mercy, and the ability to remain grounded in a world of noise.

In an age where image is often manipulated and authenticity is rare, Leo XIV's authenticity didn't need amplification. It was visible in his silence, present in his gaze, and real in his refusal to claim center stage.

Voices from His Inner Circle

To understand Pope Leo XIV, it is not enough to trace his official biography. One must also listen to the voices of those who have walked beside him: fellow priests, religious sisters, laypeople, former students, and colleagues in the Vatican. Their recollections reveal a man whose public humility is not a stylistic choice but a lifelong posture — someone formed by the quiet work of fidelity, not the spotlight of power.

"He listens as if you're the only person in the world."

This phrase, repeated by multiple people who worked with him during his years in Peru and Rome, speaks volumes. According to Sister Magdalena Pérez, a catechist in Trujillo who collaborated with then-Bishop Prevost on parish programs,

"He would walk into a room of thirty people, and within five minutes he had already noticed who hadn't spoken. Then he'd find a way to gently draw them in."

His emotional intelligence, especially his ability to read the room and to make space for others' dignity, was something that struck many. In an institution where titles often precede relationships, Prevost reversed the order. People mattered before rank.

Fellow Augustinians often describe Leo XIV not as an administrator or even a theologian first, but as a brother."He never lived above the others," recalls Fr. Tomás Rivera, a Peruvian Augustinian who shared a house with him for several years. *"He cooked, he swept, he prayed — and he never spoke more than necessary."*

Even in positions of leadership, such as when he served as Prior General of the Order, he resisted any form of clerical elitism. He made it clear that leadership should serve, not elevate.

"A man who doesn't pretend to have all the answers."

This was the description given by Archbishop Matteo Conti, who worked closely with him in the Dicastery for Bishops. Conti described how Prevost would enter meetings well-prepared, but never with closed conclusions.

"He would say, 'Let's pray first,' and then he would ask questions. Not rhetorical ones — real ones. Sometimes he'd change his view. That's rare in the Vatican."

Conti emphasized that his style wasn't uncertainty, but discernment — the deliberate refusal to rush into judgment, even on difficult episcopal appointments.

Those close to Leo XIV say he has always operated from a strong inner life, shaped by early morning prayer, a love of the Psalms, and frequent spiritual direction. His personal journals, according to one confidant, are "more full of questions than answers." He is said to frequently meditate on Augustine's writings, especially the *Confessions*, where the theme of interiority and truth recurs constantly.

His motto as bishop — *"In Veritate Servire"* ("To serve in truth") — wasn't a slogan. It was his way of being. Friends report that he often declined invitations to high-profile events in favor of visiting prisons or conducting pastoral visits in isolated communities.

"No one feared him," said one Vatican journalist after his election. *"That's not typical."*

But that doesn't mean Leo XIV is soft. Those close to him also describe a steely patience, a man who can say "no" with calm finality and who is never rushed by external pressure. He has removed priests from leadership quietly but decisively when abuse or corruption was discovered. He believes that firmness without humiliation is the Christian path.

In short, his inner circle describes him not as a saint, but as something more useful to the modern Church: a man who is trustworthy.

What Stayed and What Changed Overnight

The evening of May 8, 2025, marked a definitive break in the life of Robert Francis Prevost. In the space of a single hour, he became Pope Leo XIV — spiritual father to over 1.3 billion Catholics, head of the world's largest religious institution, and one of the most watched moral voices on the planet.

And yet, as those who knew him quickly noticed: very little changed about the man himself.

The same black shoes. The same modest watch. The same cross — made of wood and worn smooth at the edges from decades of use. The same prayer rhythm at dawn, the same handwritten notes in the margins of his breviary. His demeanor didn't shift. His language didn't inflate. His walk through the Apostolic Palace the

next morning was slow and contemplative — not
as a man taking possession of power, but as
someone entering a place he had already visited
inwardly for years.

He kept his circle small. He declined a new
personal secretary in favor of the aide who had
worked with him for years in the dicastery. He
continued to answer his own correspondence, at
least for the first few days, until the incoming
volume made it impossible.

Insiders noted that, despite now having
thousands at his command, he still made his own
coffee.

But while Leo XIV remained largely unchanged,
the world around him transformed — instantly.

Journalists scrambled to find photos of his
childhood parish in Chicago. Politicians issued
statements aligning themselves with, or
distancing themselves from, the new pope's
presumed values. Thousands flooded social
media with posts speculating on what an
"American pope" might mean for global
Catholicism. Some supporters projected him as a
moral ally for Western democracies; others
feared a culture war in cassock form.

Yet the pope himself offered no such drama. His
early choices were carefully non-sensational. He
didn't replace his predecessor's key advisors
overnight. He didn't publish an immediate policy
statement. Instead, he met quietly with refugees,
had lunch with Vatican gardeners, and spent an

afternoon in silent adoration in the chapel of St. John Paul II.

When asked by a close aide what his priority would be in the first weeks of his pontificate, Leo XIV simply answered:

 "To listen. The world is loud. The Church must first become quiet again."

What changed overnight was his visibility. What did not change was his center.

Observers sensed it: this was not a man seeking to impress the world, but a man rooted enough to resist it. The global media, still unsure how to categorize him, began calling him "the silent shepherd" — a term he neither accepted nor rejected.

Thus began the papacy of Leo XIV: not with a bang, but with a calm, steady gaze — a posture formed in Peruvian barrios, tempered in Roman corridors, and forged in the quiet pews of a Chicago parish.

The man had changed titles. But his direction had not.

II - THE ELECTION THAT SHOOK THE WORLD

The death of **Pope Francis** on **April 21, 2025**, marked a profound moment of transition for the Catholic Church. His passing on Easter Monday, following a stroke and subsequent cardiac arrest, left the Church mourning the loss of a pontiff known for his humility, commitment to social justice, and efforts to bridge divides within the global Catholic community. His 12-year papacy had been characterized by a focus on mercy, outreach to marginalized populations, and a push for reforms aimed at making the Church more inclusive and responsive to contemporary challenges.

In the wake of his death, the Church found itself at a crossroads. The faithful grappled with questions about the future direction of the papacy and the Church's role in addressing pressing global issues. The conclave convened on **May 7, 2025**, bringing together cardinals from around the world to elect a new leader who could navigate the complexities of modernity while honoring the Church's rich traditions.

In many Western countries, including the United States and much of Europe, mass attendance was declining, young people were disengaged, and many viewed the Church as either

hopelessly conservative or **too politically compromised**. Meanwhile, the global South — Latin America, Africa, parts of Asia — was becoming the vibrant center of Catholic life, yet lacked the same structural influence in Rome. There were mounting tensions:

- Between bishops who favored a synodal, consultative Church, and those who preferred hierarchical clarity.
- Between progressive voices advocating for women's roles and LGBTQ+ inclusion, and more traditional factions warning against doctrinal erosion.
- Between the Vatican Curia's administrative core and local churches demanding autonomy and reform.

Francis had initiated major changes: streamlining canon law, opening new dialogues, decentralizing some authority. But by 2025, many of those reforms were either stalled or fiercely contested. As one Vatican commentator put it, *"The house has been rearranged, but no one agrees who owns which rooms."*

Beyond the Church: A Fractured World

At the same time, the broader world seemed to mirror the Church's own fragmentation. The political climate was charged: populism surging in some regions, democratic institutions under stress, economic systems shaken by inequality and automation. Climate disasters were becoming commonplace, and wars had reemerged as realities, not relics.

In this atmosphere, the Church stood as one of the last global moral institutions still claiming universal reach. And yet, many questioned whether it had the strength to act.

That was the background to the 2025 conclave. More than the election of a new pope, it was a crossroads moment:

Would the Church double down on old patterns? Would it take a radical turn?

Or would it try something rarer still to speak quietly but clearly, with both conviction and compassion?

The answer came in the form of Leo XIV, a man not widely seen as a frontrunner, but someone whose life story had already woven through the very tensions the Church now faced.

He didn't just emerge from the conclave. He embodied its deeper longing: for leadership that is credible, rooted, and free from the need to perform.

The election of **Cardinal Robert Francis Prevost** as **Pope Leo XIV** on **May 8, 2025**, signaled a historic shift. As the first American-born pope, his ascension represented both continuity and change—a commitment to the values espoused by his predecessor, coupled with a fresh perspective shaped by his experiences in the United States and Latin

America. His election was met with a mix of hope, curiosity, and anticipation as the world watched to see how he would lead the Church into a new era.

On May 7, 2025, 124 cardinal electors filed into the Sistine Chapel beneath the thunderous fresco of Michelangelo's *Last Judgment*. The marble floors echoed softly under their red slippers; the weight of tradition, secrecy, and divine expectation pressed heavily on every movement. The world outside speculated feverishly — but inside, the tone was markedly different: solemn, attentive, patient.

This conclave came not on the heels of resignation, but after the death of a beloved pope. Pope Francis's final year had been marked by declining health but continued moral clarity, and his Easter Sunday benediction, just hours before his passing became a kind of living testament. His absence was now felt not only as a loss of leadership but as a spiritual void.

The Weight of History

Each cardinal took the oath of secrecy, swearing before the crucifix and gospel that they would not reveal what would unfold in the chapel. Mobile phones were sealed away. External contact was forbidden. The centuries-old rituals began: the chanting *"Veni Creator Spiritus"*, the ritual lock of the doors — the Church literally and symbolically closing itself off from the world to better hear God's whisper.

Many of the cardinals had come with assumptions: favorites, coalitions, even informal lobbying. But as in every conclave, once the door closed and the ballots began, those assumptions started to shift in the face of silence.

"You feel your ego shrink," one participant would later say anonymously. "You are no longer a bishop, or a theologian, or a national representative. You are a soul before God, and you are being asked to listen."

The Candidates:

Initial speculation centered on a few prominent figures:

- A cardinal from the Philippines, seen as a charismatic bridge between East and West.
- An Italian archbishop known for his theological precision and doctrinal orthodoxy.
- A Latin American cardinal, close to Francis, representing continuity.

But by the end of the first day, whispers began to circulate about a "consensus figure" — someone respected by all camps but aligned with none. A man who had no known enemies, who had governed quietly, served faithfully, and led with a kind of gentle firmness that many found deeply credible.

Cardinal Robert Francis Prevost.

He wasn't part of any campaign. He hadn't published position papers. He had never been described as a "papabile" by mainstream analysts. And yet, he began to draw votes from the second round onward.

The decision did not emerge as a result of clever maneuvering or ideological compromise. Several cardinals would later describe the experience as one of spiritual convergence. One senior African cardinal was quoted (again anonymously) as saying:

"I voted for him not because he was American, but because he was the only one I knew would speak to both Rome and the peripheries."

By the fourth ballot, the majority had been reached. The vote count was precise, but the mood was not celebratory. It was still, almost reverent. A simple question was asked:

"Do you accept your election?"

Cardinal Prevost reportedly paused, closed his eyes for a long moment, and answered:

"I accept. In faith and in weakness."

When asked what name he would take, his answer surprised some, but not all:

"Leo"

A murmur passed through the room and then, stillness again.

Turning Point – What the Church Chose

When the white smoke rose over the Vatican on May 8, 2025, the world saw a new pontiff. But within the Church, something more subtle happened: it was not just the election of a new pope — it was the revealing of the Church's own self-image at a time of deep transition.

The choice of Cardinal Robert Francis Prevost - now Leo XIV- was not the most obvious or predictable decision. But in hindsight, it was deeply revealing. A Church Choosing Pastoral Authority Over Public Theater.

In an age when visibility is often mistaken for vision, the Church chose a man who had built no brand, made no public bids for leadership, and gave few interviews. The cardinals did not choose a firebrand, a media-savvy diplomat, or a high-profile doctrinal enforcer. They chose a man known for his reliability, discernment, and moral steadiness.

The message was clear: the Church did not want more spectacle. It wanted credibility. It did not want another performer. It wanted a pastor.

Leo XIV's election said: authenticity is enough.

A Church That Remembered the Global South. Though Leo XIV holds an American passport, his election was not a victory for the Western Church. Quite the opposite. His spiritual biography was shaped by Trujillo, not Washington. His theology matured in Latin America. His pastoral instincts were honed among the poor, the rural, the forgotten. In choosing him, the cardinals made a quiet but radical statement:

"The Church's future is not where its wealth is. It's where its wounds are."

His voice, formed in barrios and prayer rooms, resonated because it was free of imperial tone, sensitive to complexity, and attuned to suffering.

Leo XIV was neither a progressive lightning rod nor a conservative fallback. And this, too, was telling. The Church did not elect someone to win a cultural war within its walls. Instead, it chose someone who might quiet the conflict without silencing the questions.

The decision reflected a weariness with polarization and an appetite for synthesis — someone who could honor tradition without rigidity, and listen to change without losing theological center.

In Leo XIV, the cardinals recognized a man who could say no without cruelty, and yes without dilution. That balance, though difficult to define, was precisely what the Church needed — and, evidently, chose.

Perhaps most significant was this: by electing Leo XIV, the Church resisted the urge to respond to the world's chaos with speed. It did not select a political actor to play global chess. It did not rush to make headlines. It chose, instead, a contemplative leader in a culture of compulsive reaction.

May 8 thus became more than a change of name. It became a recalibration of the Church's voice.

Not louder. Just clearer.
Not newer. Just more faithful.
Not safer. Just deeper.

How Leo XIV is Redefining His Own Legacy

When Cardinal Prevost chose the name Leo XIV, the Vatican's historical commentators immediately reached for analogies: Leo XIII the social reformer, Leo I the Great, the "lion of doctrine and diplomacy." But while such parallels are useful, they only tell part of the story.

In the early days of his pontificate, Pope Leo XIV has shown little interest in being defined by history. Instead, he is using his name as a lens -not a script. And what has emerged is a new kind of papal style: neither monarchic nor managerial, but something more difficult to pin down- and perhaps more necessary than either.

The name "Leo" evokes strength. But Leo XIV's strength is not loud or demonstrative. It manifests in his ability to withhold, to wait, to choose the moment. His first public gestures -visiting a children's hospice before holding a press conference, declining luxury accommodations, remaining silent for long stretches in prayer- have all suggested a redefinition of papal authority.

He is not seeking to rule like a lion, but to protect like one — guarding the vulnerable, standing watch over unity, sensing danger before others speak of it.

In this way, Leo XIV is writing his own meaning into the name.

Unlike Leo XIII, who wielded encyclicals like surgical instruments, Leo XIV has not yet issued a major document. And unlike Leo I, who spoke with rhetorical thunder to emperors and invaders, Leo XIV's public language is careful, almost hesitant. But that hesitancy is not weakness. It is ethical restraint.

In his first homily to the College of Cardinals, he reportedly said:

"If a voice is to matter, it must first learn silence."

This suggests a papacy not defined by productivity or press cycles, but by a slower moral arc.

By choosing "Leo," Prevost placed himself in continuity with a papal tradition of muscular clarity. But his way of enacting that clarity is not through confrontation or assertion. It's through presence, memory, and mercy.

His use of the name becomes less about reclaiming historical glory and more about retrieving the courage to be pastoral in a time of institutional fragility.

For many Catholics around the world, especially those alienated by ideology, bureaucracy, or moralism, this change in tone is more than style. It is substance.

Leo XIV is not performing a legacy. He is planting one.

And with each understated move, he reminds the Church that strength is not in dominance, but in devotion — especially when devotion remains quiet under pressure.

Global South Watch – Hopes from the Peripheries

When Leo XIV stepped out onto the balcony in St. Peter's Square, Catholics in Lima, Kigali, Manila, and Kinshasa were not asking what this new pope meant for Western geopolitics. They were asking something more direct, more pastoral:

"Will he remember us now that he is in Rome?"

For much of the Global South, the papacy has often felt far away - not in faith, but in structure. The Vatican's tone, vocabulary, and governance have long echoed the rhythms of Europe. Even as Catholicism's numerical center of gravity shifted southward, the symbolic and administrative weight remained in the North.

Leo XIV's election didn't end that imbalance - but it changed the emotional calculus. He was not born in the South. But he had lived there. Learned there. Suffered with it. Prayed in its languages. Buried its dead.

In Peru, where Leo XIV served for decades, the response was more than political—it was familial. He had baptized children, consoled grieving mothers, ministered in flooded villages and gang-ridden neighborhoods. Now he was pope. And yet in interviews across Trujillo and Chiclayo, people referred to him still as *"Padre Roberto."*

Catholics there expressed not just pride, but a moral claim:

"We know how he listens. Now the whole Church will hear what we heard."

In Brazil, Colombia, and Argentina, his election revived hope that the Church would speak not only with dogma, but with intimacy - addressing poverty, exclusion, and ecological justice not as theories, but as wounds they had bled from.

In parts of sub-Saharan Africa, Leo XIV's early gestures - his modesty, his silence, his emphasis on service — resonated strongly with a growing generation of bishops and lay leaders seeking to model the Gospel without clerical elitism. One Nigerian priest put it this way:

"He wears his white robe like a fieldworker, not a prince."

His non-European background in style and spirituality offered an unexpected kinship. He may not have served in Africa, but he carried a non-imperial ecclesiology - one shaped more by walking than by ruling.

Across parts of Asia, particularly in the Philippines and India, Leo XIV's election was seen as a signal that the Church might finally embrace cultural particularity without apology. His refusal to centralize immediately, his prioritization of listening before legislating, offered hope that local expressions of Catholicism would be taken more seriously.

For many in Asia, where interreligious dialogue and minority Catholic identity shape daily reality, Leo XIV's Augustinian inner gaze seemed better suited to navigating complexity than confrontation.

More Than Representation

What the Global South hopes for in Leo XIV is not a papacy **about** them. It is a papacy that **includes** them — **as equals, as sources of wisdom, as co-creators of the Church's future**.

And in his silence, they hear something familiar.

Not indifference.
But reverence.

For the United States, the election of Leo XIV was not just a moment of pride. It was also, and perhaps more uncomfortably, a mirror.
Here was a man formed in Chicago, fluent in English and Spanish, familiar with American cities and rural margins - suddenly placed in a role that gave him enormous moral authority. Not as a partisan, not as a pundit, not as a Supreme Court nominee. As the pope.
And that raised an implicit question for American Catholics — and American culture more broadly:
What does it mean when someone shaped by your society returns as your conscience?

A Nation of Catholic Contradictions
America has long been a paradox for the Catholic Church. It is home to:

- One of the largest Catholic populations in the world
- Some of the most polarized intra-Church debates
- Deep philanthropic generosity
- And a widening moral distrust in institutional religion

Catholicism in the U.S. today is deeply split between "culture warrior" conservatism and "activist" progressivism, with many ordinary Catholics caught in a middle that no longer speaks loudly enough.

Leo XIV did not emerge from either camp. And that's what made his election so startling. He was not a flag-bearer for a faction. He was a return to an older model of Christian maturity: pastoral, patient, intellectually serious, spiritually consistent.

For some Americans, this was reassuring. For others, it was quietly unsettling.

He Doesn't Fit the Algorithm.

In a culture driven by fast takes, cable news cycles, and ideological branding, Leo XIV's first weeks offered none of the usual cues. He did not wade into domestic politics. He didn't endorse legislative battles. He didn't invoke national identity. He simply prayed, listened, and pointed back to the Gospel.

This has made him difficult to claim - and even harder to dismiss. He doesn't belong to the left or the right. He speaks calmly in a world that rewards outrage. He invokes virtue when others demand victory.

In this way, Leo XIV is less a leader for America than a lesson to it: that spiritual authority is not about noise, but about rootedness.

A Challenge to all sides

- For conservatives who equate holiness with moral rigidity, Leo XIV is a disruption: he is firm in principle, but gentle in tone.
- For progressives who expect structural revolution, he is a disappointment: slow-moving, methodical, reluctant to politicize.
- For centrists, he is a quiet test of conscience: will they follow a leader who asks for depth, not comfort?

He is, in essence, a Catholic Pope - not an American one.

But in being Catholic, he becomes most useful to America. Because he shows a path out of the false binaries — and into something older, truer, and more demanding.

Leo XIV does not represent America. He represents the Church. But from that vantage point, he reflects America back to itself: fractured, anxious, hopeful, capable of renewal - if it is willing to listen again to voices that don't need to shout.

The Papacy and the Age of Mistrust

The modern papacy was born in an era of sacred authority and clear institutional confidence. That world no longer exists.

In 2025, trust in institutions is near historic lows - not just in governments or corporations, but in religious bodies, media, academia, even science.

Authority figures are often regarded with suspicion. Leaders are judged more by soundbites than substance. And transparency, while necessary, has sometimes replaced truth with volatility.

The Church has not been spared. Decades of abuse scandals, financial opacity, doctrinal whiplash, and factionalism have left deep scars. For many Catholics, especially in the West, the institution no longer feels like a guardian of the faith but a fragile vessel barely holding together.

A New Papacy in a Distrustful Age

Into this environment stepped Pope Leo XIV - a man who neither radiates charisma nor brandishes ideological clarity. His early actions have been understated. His voice is measured, sometimes hesitant. Yet it is precisely this difference that has drawn attention.

In an age where most institutions feel forced to shout in order to be heard, Leo XIV has done the opposite. He has shown no instinct to defend the Church's prestige, and no rush to assert personal vision. Instead, he has started with something radically rare in public life: trusting the people by not manipulating them.

He does not flatter. He does not panic. He does not conceal that the Church is wounded.

"I believe in truth that walks," he told a small gathering of priests in one of his first private audiences.

"It stumbles sometimes, but it moves forward."

Leo XIV's refusal to dramatize has had consequences. Some accuse him of being too passive. Others, of lacking urgency. There is a sense among certain Vatican insiders that the media is not "excited enough" about him.

But he seems uninterested in manufactured impact. Instead, he has allowed his credibility to rest on a longer rhythm: consistency, patience, and integrity over time.

He is not trying to rebuild the Church's reputation through campaign strategy. He is attempting something deeper: to rebuild the moral imagination from the inside out.

That is slow work. But it may be the only kind of work that can outlast a crisis of trust.

One striking early shift under Leo XIV has been the tone of Vatican communication. There are fewer press bulletins. More silence between statements. A noticeable shift from reactive posture to interior depth. This is not a lack of openness, but a refusal to perform clarity where there is none.

In a world that expects leaders to explain everything immediately, Leo XIV has started by asking better questions - and showing his willingness to sit with them.

He has, in effect, refused to exploit the papacy for institutional defense. Instead, he has offered the one thing the modern world rarely sees in high office: a public figure who speaks less so that others might hear more.

While commentators speculated, bishops published statements, and journalists scrambled for narratives, something quieter was happening in parishes, living rooms, and chapels around the world.

Ordinary Catholics were watching. Not analyzing. Not dissecting. Just watching.

And many of them — those who had long felt forgotten by Church politics and left behind by ideological battles — began to breathe a little more easily.

In dozens of interviews conducted in the weeks after Leo the Fourteenth's election, parish priests and lay ministers reported a similar theme. Parishioners — many of whom had grown weary of both scandal and spectacle — expressed a cautious sense of recognition.

They were not looking for a celebrity pope. They were looking for someone who felt real.

"He seems like someone who knows what it means to sit in the back pew," one woman in Milwaukee told her priest.

"He does not act like he owns the Church. He acts like he belongs to it".

This was not naïve idealism. It was quiet relief. A feeling that the highest office in the Church might finally reflect the tone so many faithful Catholics try to live every day — humble, consistent, rooted in prayer rather than opinion.

Among many ordinary believers, there is a growing fatigue with extremes. One side shouts about doctrinal decay. The other demands institutional revolution. In between are millions who go to Sunday Mass, care for elderly parents, and try to raise their children with some sense of sacred order.

Leo the Fourteenth does not speak directly to this middle. He does not need to. He inhabits it.

He does not fuel the battles that drain parish life. He neither provokes nor apologizes for Catholic identity. Instead, he simply acts as if the faith is real — not an argument to be won, but a path to be walked.

This simplicity, after years of high-stakes Church drama, feels like peace.

One parish in São Paulo reported a surge in confessions the week after the new pope's election. A diocesan newsletter in Manila noted renewed interest in Eucharistic adoration. A priest in Lyon said parishioners told him they were "just glad to see a pope who does not want to talk all the time."

Leo the Fourteenth has made no sweeping doctrinal declarations. But already, in his posture and presence, he is re-centering the Catholic imagination.

He has not told the Church what to believe. He has reminded it how to believe - gently, patiently, and with both feet on the ground.

This is not a revival of ideology. It is a return to something older and quieter. Something many had been waiting for without knowing how to name it.

Now they have a name. And it is Leo.

Rome Without Drama

Inside the walls of the Apostolic Palace, a shift has taken place. It is not loud, not formal, and not revolutionary. But it is real.

The early days of Leo the Fourteenth's pontificate have marked a noticeable change in the tone of Vatican governance. Gone are the dramatic appointments, grand statements, and abrupt restructuring. In their place is something unusual for a global institution: calm administrative consistency.

From the beginning, Leo the Fourteenth made it clear that he would not rush. He retained many members of the Curia who had served under Francis. He refused to replace key officials until he had met with them personally and understood the full picture. This sent a quiet message through the corridors of the Vatican: loyalty would not be judged by political alignment, but by integrity and depth of service.

Several long-standing departments reported that the new pope asked only two questions in their initial private audiences:

"What are you doing that is working?"

"What are you doing because it has always been done that way?"

This was not a test. It was an invitation to reflect. And many insiders said they had never felt more listened to.

Previous popes had close circles of advisers, often old friends or academic confidants. Leo the Fourteenth appears to operate differently. He has chosen not to centralize decision-making in a single group. Instead, he holds brief, focused conversations with people from different backgrounds and regions. He has emphasized diversity of experience over ideological conformity.

A source close to the Secretariat of State noted,

"He does not ask what you think. He asks how you know what you think."

This kind of questioning has slowed some processes, but it has also lowered internal tension. The feeling in many offices is that there is now space to breathe, to think, to adjust without fear of political fallout.

Despite his reflective style, Leo the Fourteenth is not indecisive. On matters where clarity is needed, he acts. In the case of a bishop accused of financial misconduct, he requested an investigation within days of taking office. But he refused to comment publicly until the facts were verified.

When asked why he had not issued any major statements about Church governance, he is reported to have said,

"I do not need to speak until I am sure I am not just speaking to be heard."

This careful approach may frustrate commentators. But inside the Vatican, it has begun to restore something more valuable than headlines: trust in the rhythm of discernment.

In choosing calm over urgency, reflection over reaction, Leo the Fourteenth is not weakening the papacy. He is giving it back its center.

A new pope always inherits not just a Church, but a climate. The tone, pace, and focus of his first weeks send quiet but powerful messages. Even when no formal declarations are issued, appointments and silences begin to shape the new order.

In the case of Leo the Fourteenth, these early signals have not been loud. But they have been unmistakable.

One of the most surprising decisions — or rather, non-decisions — has been his willingness to maintain continuity. Many observers expected an immediate reshuffling of Vatican positions. Instead, Leo has left key figures from the Francis era in place, while quietly observing their work and inviting private conversation.

His first major act was not to reassign leadership. It was to visit a community of disabled children on the outskirts of Rome, away from the cameras. The signal was clear: reform would begin with attention, not announcement.

By not drawing harsh lines between his own leadership and that of his predecessor, Leo has chosen a path of respectful succession, one that neither halts reform nor exaggerates it. This places him not in the center of a debate, but above it - focused more on what serves the people of God than what pleases headlines.

Where he has made new appointments, they speak volumes. He has chosen bishops who are pastoral rather than ideological. One recent archbishop in West Africa is known for his work with trauma survivors, not for theological writing. Another in Central Europe is a former prison chaplain. Neither has written public manifestos. Both are widely loved by their communities.

When asked in private what he looks for in leadership, Leo is said to have answered with a single sentence:

"I trust those who are trusted by the poor."

This does not mean he ignores theology or canon law. But it does mean that service, not style, is becoming the foundation for authority.

Some assumed Leo the Fourteenth would simply carry on the legacy of Francis. Others feared he would undo it. In truth, he is doing neither.

Where Francis disrupted institutional habits, Leo seems to quietly realign them. Where Francis was prophet and challenger, Leo seems to be gardener and guide. His respect for the previous papacy is clear, but so is his desire to slow the pace and deepen the roots. He is not building something new. He is tending what has already begun to grow.

No pope steps into the role without carrying the hopes of others. But in the case of Leo the Fourteenth, the expectations are especially layered.

He arrives at a time when the Church is not only divided, but tired — tired of scandal, tired of arguing, tired of waiting for something to change. And now, in his calm, steady posture, many see a new beginning. Perhaps too much.

For some, Leo is expected to complete what Pope Francis started: to bring the Church into full accountability, decentralize authority, and make it truly inclusive. For others, he is hoped to restore discipline, clarity, and a firmer sense of theological identity.

In every corner of the Church, there are voices saying, Some want a statement on gender. Others call for a new response to abuse. Some expect reform of the Roman Curia. Others want a revival of sacred liturgy. The calendar is filling with invitations, proposals, and requests.

Yet Leo the Fourteenth has not shown signs of haste. His early moves have been careful, even restrained. He listens, absorbs, and speaks little. But the pressure is real. More than once in history, popes have become symbols for things they did not choose. Some were claimed by reformers they did not fully support. Others were imagined as traditionalists because they remained silent.

Leo now faces this risk as well. His simplicity may be read as softness. His silence may be mistaken for indecision. His patience may be misinterpreted as avoidance.

The real challenge will not be in choosing policies. It will be in resisting the temptation to become what others need him to be rather than what he is called to be.

The Fragility of the Moment

There are moments in history when institutions become louder to protect themselves. And there are other moments when they become quiet because something more subtle is happening — something uncertain, maybe sacred. The Catholic Church is now living in such a moment.

The election of Leo the Fourteenth has not launched a revolution. It has not triggered backlash or rejoicing. It has, instead, created a pause — a delicate pause. A kind of spiritual stillness that could either become renewal or evaporate under pressure.

The Church is not crumbling. But it is tender. It has wounds that are not yet closed, divisions that have not yet healed, and hopes that are not yet clear.

Leo has not offered grand visions. He has offered presence. And presence is harder to grasp than policy. It does not reassure with guarantees. It only invites. And so the Church stands now in a kind of threshold space — between distrust and trust, between performance and prayer, between fear and possibility.

Many faithful sense it, even if they cannot name it. A parish priest in Marseille recently said,

"It feels like we are all exhaling for the first time in years. But we are not yet breathing freely."

Fragility is not failure. But it is sensitive to force. If the Church moves too quickly to define this papacy, if critics or supporters force Leo to respond before he is ready, the quiet clarity he has begun to build may not hold.

There is a danger in rushing to decide what this pontificate must mean. The grace of this moment is that it remains undefined. The danger is that the world may not have the patience to wait for it to unfold.

Pope Leo may be prepared to walk slowly. The question is whether we are prepared to follow slowly, too.

In every fragile moment, there is also the possibility of something beautiful. A fragile branch can bloom. A quiet pause can become prayer. A leader who does not hurry can invite a people who do not panic.

Leo the Fourteenth is not asking the Church to believe in him. He is asking it to remember what it believes. That God works in silence. That truth is patient. That holiness begins not in momentum, but in mercy.

This is a fragile moment. But fragility is not weakness.
It may be the first real sign of strength the Church has shown in years.

A New Kind of Strength

In the history of the Church, popes have often come to symbolize an era. Some were reformers. Others were theologians. A few were diplomats or defenders of orthodoxy. They led with force, with intellect, or with institutional clarity. Their strength was easy to describe.

Pope Leo the Fourteenth represents something more difficult to define, but no less powerful. He stands not as the leader of a program or the center of a faction. He stands as a witness to an older strength - the kind that does not need to declare itself.

There is strength in public presence. But there is also strength in waiting. There is strength in visibility. But there is greater strength in restraint. Leo the Fourteenth represents a form of leadership that does not seek to impress, but to endure. It does not seek to direct attention, but to redirect it toward what matters.

This is a strength that listens more than it speaks, that carries history without using it as a weapon, that holds space for others without losing its own form. It is spiritual maturity in action.

Much has been made of Leo's slow pace, his cautious tone, his refusal to define his papacy too soon. But this, too, is a kind of strength. To resist the demands of narrative. To remain firm in prayer while others write headlines. To disappoint those who want him to move faster, not because he is unwilling, but because he is attentive to something deeper than urgency. There is courage in clarity. But there is also courage in silence. Especially when the world does not understand it.

More than anything else, Leo the Fourteenth represents the return of hope that is not naive. His hope is not in applause or renewal by strategy. It is in grace. It is in patience. It is in God.

This is the kind of hope the Church has often forgotten in moments of crisis - the hope that does not shout, but stands. That does not fix, but accompanies. That does not need to prove itself, because it trusts what cannot yet be seen.

In Leo the Fourteenth, the Church does not have a strongman. It has a steady man. And in this age, that may be the strongest kind of leader it could have hoped for.

III - QUIET REVOLUTION BEGINS

In the weeks after the election of Leo the Fourteenth, something began to shift within the Catholic Church. It was not dramatic. There were no sweeping reforms or sudden declarations. But across parishes, seminaries, religious houses, and chancery offices, a new tone was quietly taking shape.

It was a change not in doctrine, but in disposition.

Not in structure, but in spirit.

Priests who had spent years treading carefully in a climate of liturgical conflict began to preach more freely — not because they felt emboldened, but because they felt less watched.

Catechists who had grown weary of ideological language began to focus again on questions of mercy, of meaning, of the interior life.

Bishops, previously cautious about being perceived as partisan, began to rediscover pastoral presence as a form of courage, not compromise.

It is worth noting that Leo the Fourteenth had not sent out a single document to cause this shift. He had not issued any new norms, called for reforms, or made sweeping judgments about the Church's direction.

And yet, the effect was real. In many parts of the world, it felt as though the Church had exhaled.
A young priest in Kraków described it this way:
"It is as if we are being allowed to be ourselves agai - not to perform the Church, but to live it."
What Leo has introduced is not a program. It is a posture. One that encourages calm instead of urgency, listening instead of reaction, presence instead of performance.
This change in tone has begun to spread, not through decree, but through recognition. The people of the Church are seeing in the pope something familiar - not because they knew him, but because they know what it means to be faithful without spectacle, to love the Gospel without seeking control.
In seeing that spirit in the highest office, they are rediscovering it in themselves.
This shift is not only emotional. It is beginning to shape how diocesan offices prioritize formation. How bishops communicate. How theological faculty approach questions of disagreement.
It is still early. The waters have not fully moved. But something deeper is beginning to flow.

Leo the Fourteenth has not pushed the Church in a new direction.
He has reminded it of the direction it always claimed to follow.
And that quiet reminder is already becoming movement.

One of the clearest signs of a new papal direction is how bishops begin to move.

Not through formal declarations. Not through public speeches. But through posture. Through emphasis. Through the tone they take when they speak to their priests, their seminarians, their people. Under Pope Leo the Fourteenth, a noticeable shift is unfolding in the way many bishops now carry their office. In the years leading up to this pontificate, many bishops felt trapped between public expectation and internal conflict. To speak too directly risked controversy. To remain silent invited suspicion. Some became cautious managers. Others defaulted to ideological rhetoric. Very few seemed free.

Now, something is changing.

In diocesan communications and clergy meetings, bishops have begun to speak with less polish and more presence. They are naming wounds without fearing headlines. They are asking more questions than they answer. Some are even admitting uncertainty without the usual caveats.

This is not a collapse of leadership. It is a restoration of its human side. The model offered by Leo the Fourteenth - measured, attentive, modest in appearance - is beginning to give bishops permission to govern without pretense.

In South Korea, a bishop known for strict administrative control recently initiated a monthly listening session with lay ministers. In the United

Kingdom, a bishop who had previously focused on public apologetics gave a talk on spiritual dryness — his own included. In Mexico, a newly ordained bishop visited every prison in his diocese before writing a pastoral letter.

None of these changes were ordered by Rome. But all of them reflect a climate shift.

What is also notable is that this shift is not only taking place in the global South or among young bishops. It is happening across regions and generations. Senior bishops who served under three or more popes are adjusting their language. Some who once distanced themselves from Francis's reforms are now reconsidering the meaning of presence and tone. Not because they have changed doctrine, but because they are sensing a change in rhythm - and it is one they understand. They have seen how Leo leads. And they recognize the strength in his gentleness. They remember what it means to serve before speaking. This quiet repositioning is not yet dramatic. There are still dioceses where fear controls decisions, and others where ideology dominates. But more and more bishops are finding a kind of middle ground — a place where tradition and reform are no longer posed as enemies, and where silence is not seen as absence.

What Leo the Fourteenth has given them is not a new model to imitate. He has given them permission to lead from their own depth, not from institutional pressure.

The Renewal of Formation Culture

For years, many Catholic seminaries have mirrored the Church's broader tensions. Some became enclaves of theological resistance, where candidates were trained to defend a threatened orthodoxy. Others turned toward therapeutic models of discernment, often without spiritual depth. Between them stood a generation of seminarians often more concerned with surviving the formation process than being formed by it.

With the election of Leo the Fourteenth, something is beginning to shift. Not through mandates or reforms, but through tone. And nowhere is that shift more subtle or more significant than in the places where future priests are learning to listen to God.

Seminary rectors across multiple continents have reported a quiet change in how students speak of the papacy. Under previous pontificates, seminarian cultures often reflected the polarities of the wider Church. Popes were viewed as banners for liturgical preference or doctrinal security. Now, for the first time in many years, many seminarians are beginning to speak of the pope not as a symbol but as a spiritual reference point.

A rector in the Philippines noted,
"The questions we hear now are less about vestments and more about how to stay rooted in pastoral life."
This does not signal a loss of tradition. It signals the return of a formation mindset that is interested in the interior life, not just the exterior performance of priesthood. One of the most discussed changes is the reemergence of silent prayer in many houses of formation. Some seminaries have reinstated weekly periods of extended Eucharistic adoration. Others have begun to teach contemplative prayer as a core discipline, not just an optional enrichment.
This movement has not come from above. It has risen from below — from students who see in Leo the Fourteenth a model of steady, interior strength, and who wish to cultivate that same stillness in themselves.
Formation directors have begun to report fewer disciplinary cases, more self-awareness, and a notable shift in the emotional tone of daily seminary life.

One formator in France put it simply:
"The noise is fading. We are hearing each other again."

Another change is taking shape in how future priests are learning to imagine their role.

The model of priest as public defender of truth, often shaped more by media than theology, is giving way to a model drawn from the daily life of Leo the Fourteenth. Seminarians are beginning to speak about the priesthood as presence rather than platform. They are noticing that their pope does not dominate the conversation. He makes room. And that example is beginning to reshape how they want to walk into a parish for the first time — not as a voice of control, but as a steady presence in a vulnerable community.

The renewal of seminary culture is not complete.
But it has begun.
And what guides it is not a curriculum or decree.
It is a man who leads not by example alone, but
*by the quiet **gravity of a soul that listens**.*

In the first weeks of Pope Leo the Fourteenth's pontificate, much of the global attention focused on bishops, public statements, and the changing tone of Church governance. But far from the headlines and ceremonies, a quieter resonance has taken root — within the cloisters and monastic chapels of the Church.

Contemplative religious communities, often overlooked in institutional analysis, are beginning to speak of this papacy with a rare sense of kinship.

Not because Leo has spoken directly to them. But because he reflects something they have always known. In letters, interviews, and spiritual conferences, monks and nuns across multiple continents have described Leo's silence as familiar. His restraint, his reluctance to explain himself, his gentle approach to authority — all of this mirrors what many contemplative communities have lived for generations.

A Benedictine abbot in Spain said it this way:
"He is governing like someone who has prayed for a long time."

For religious who have often felt marginal to the institutional Church, this is not merely comforting. It is spiritually affirming. Leo the Fourteenth leads with what they themselves hold sacred - stillness, inner attention, and depth over visibility. Many communities of sisters and brothers have taken this new papacy as an invitation to renew their own vocation. A Carmelite convent in Argentina added an hour of silent adoration each week in spiritual solidarity with the pope. A Trappist monastery in Kenya began a new novitiate program focused on stability and interiority. These are not programmatic reforms. They are responses of love. They are signs that the contemplative heart of the Church is awakening again, because it feels understood, even if no one has named it.
For decades, many religious felt increasingly peripheral to the life of the Church. They

watched as conferences and councils focused on activism, policy, or administration. While some engaged these movements with energy, many others felt forgotten — spoken of, but not listened to.

With Leo the Fourteenth, that sense of distance has lessened. Without visiting monasteries or publishing messages, he has conveyed through his demeanor that the Church's soul still includes the hidden life.

"He is not distracted," wrote a Poor Clare sister in Sicily.

"He knows God is the one who works."

That conviction has stirred something deep. It has reminded religious communities that their silence still has a place in the Church's future.

This is not just a matter of encouragement. It is an invitation to recover the balance between action and contemplation - a balance that, when held rightly, becomes the very rhythm of the Church's life. Leo has not told contemplatives what to do. But by being who he is, he has shown them that the Church still depends on what they offer - not in public, but in prayer.

The Return of the Ordinary

Change in the Church often begins at the top or at the margins. But the heart of Catholic life lives somewhere in between — in parishes, where people pray, gather, serve, and sometimes struggle to believe.

Parish life is rarely shaped by papal documents. It is shaped by rhythm, repetition, and relationship. That is why any shift that reaches the parish level must pass through more than headlines. It must filter down slowly, until it begins to shape how people speak to one another, how they celebrate Mass, how they imagine the Church itself.

That slow shift has begun. And Pope Leo the Fourteenth, without trying to provoke it, is beginning to influence how parishes understand what it means to belong again. In pastoral councils and ministry circles, priests and lay leaders are noting a subtle shift in tone. Instead of urgent conversations about institutional decline or growth metrics, there is a renewed focus on presence.

Parishes are asking not only how to attract people, but how to attend to those already there. Homilies have become more personal. Bulletin messages have become less promotional and more reflective.

One pastor in Canada said,

"We are less afraid of being quiet now. We are less afraid of saying we do not have every answer."

This is not because Leo issued a decree. It is because his tone has made a different kind of authority imaginable. Some of the most noticeable changes are in the most ordinary things.

More time in silence during liturgy. Fewer announcements. Increased time for confession and eucharistic adoration. A renewed interest in prayer groups, spiritual reading circles, and simple works of mercy.

In one parish in Nigeria, the catechists began visiting the sick again with regularity, something they had not done consistently since the pandemic. In a parish in Poland, the choir director reintroduced chants for quiet reflection between readings. In Chile, a youth group cancelled a social media outreach campaign and instead began visiting elderly parishioners.

These are small gestures. But they mark a change in direction. For years, many parishes have lived with quiet fear — fear of decline, of criticism, of irrelevance. That fear shaped how ministries were presented, how leaders communicated, and how faith was expressed.

Under Leo the Fourteenth, something more grounded is emerging.

His example gives permission to slow down. To speak less. To mean more. It gives parishes space to rediscover that faith is not about managing a message, but about creating a place where God can be encountered without noise.

The poor, the sick, the displaced, the lonely — they have always had a way of hearing the difference between real care and polite attention. Their experience of the Church is not filtered through academic analysis or institutional language. It is visceral. It is simple. It is direct.
And now, as Pope **Leo the Fourteenth** begins his ministry, these same people are hearing something in his voice. Something different.
Not because he promises to fix the world. But because he does not speak as if he is above it.

What Silence Sounds Like to the Poor

Many popes have spoken on behalf of the poor. Some have visited slums, refugee camps, and war zones. Others have made social justice a pillar of their message. But Leo the Fourteenth is being received differently — not for what he says, but for what he seems to understand without saying.

A nun who works with women in recovery in Brazil said it this way:

"He looks like someone who would sit with you and not be afraid of your story."

A migrant community in Spain celebrated a Mass of thanksgiving after his election, even though none of them had ever heard him speak. When asked why, one man answered,

"Because he reminds me of my grandfather. And my grandfather was the only person who never judged me."

These are not theological arguments. They are recognitions of presence. The poor often do not benefit from Church programs. They are told about them, but rarely included in their design. What reaches them more often is tone. It is the face of the priest. The gaze of the sister. The unspoken message of whether they are being tolerated or welcomed.

What many are noticing in Leo the Fourteenth is not a man trying to lead the poor. It is a man who knows how to sit next to them.

In Manila, a shelter hung a picture of him with candles around it. In rural Mexico, a priest reported that families who rarely speak of Church hierarchy began using the word "our pope" again. In South Sudan, a group of young people painted a mural of him under the words,

"He knows us."

This recognition is not without risk. The more the poor sense that Leo is one of them, the more others may try to shape his papacy through expectation or idealism. But the hope that he inspires among the forgotten does not come from policies. It comes from his refusal to speak from above.

He does not command sympathy. He allows himself to be seen.

That is why those on the margins are responding — not as activists, not as analysts, but as human beings who recognize in him a man who does not flinch at their wounds.

Silence is not an absence. It is a presence beyond sound. And for those who have lived their lives in the shadow of decisions made by others — the poor, the wounded, the forgotten — silence can become a threshold. It is where dignity is either denied or revealed.

In the presence of true silence, something long excluded is allowed to emerge: the sense of being seen without being managed, regarded without being explained. When Pope Leo the Fourteenth stepped into the light without performing power, his silence unsettled the familiar grammar of leadership. He offered no assertion. He allowed space. In doing so, he reversed the usual posture of attention: it was not the poor who had to prove their worthiness to be noticed, but the Church who chose to become quiet enough to notice them.

This kind of silence does not reduce. It does not render invisible. On the contrary, it suspends the need to be useful, and in that suspension, it permits something sacred to occur. A person who is often handled, spoken over, or condescended to finds, perhaps for the first time, that they are not being drawn into a transaction. They are simply being given back to themselves.

It is not the silence of bureaucracy, nor the cold indifference of detachment. It is not the silence that says nothing because it has nothing to say. Rather, it is the silence that knows words cannot carry what the human person is. It is the silence that has looked long enough into suffering to learn reverence.

This is why, in the early days of Leo the Fourteenth's pontificate, the response from those who have nothing has been quiet but profound. They are not reacting to a policy. They are recognizing a posture — one they understand more intuitively than the comfortable ever could.

For the poor, silence is not unfamiliar. It is what they inhabit when the world moves too quickly to notice them. But when that silence is returned to them by a figure who does not seek to escape it, it becomes something else. It becomes recognition. It becomes shelter. What the poor hear in the silence of this pope is not absence. They hear the possibility of communion. A space where they are not preached at, not diagnosed, not disciplined — but permitted to exist without shame, without translation, without fear.

The Media Takes a Breath

Contemporary media does not function well without movement. It relies on tension, contrast, escalation. Headlines must anticipate or react. Analysis must name patterns, predict motives, or expose fault lines. The modern news cycle does not observe. It accelerates.

In this environment, the election of a pope is normally a short-lived peak of interest. Speculation before the conclave, instant judgments afterward, a few days of analysis, and then a return to larger geopolitical or cultural narratives.

But something unusual has happened with Pope Leo the Fourteenth. He has not extended the media moment. He has dissolved it.

He has done this not through antagonism or avoidance, but through a refusal to provide the expected material. No controversial appointments. No sweeping public claims. No cultural alignment. No visible conflict. What remains is not drama, but space. And the media, which depends on clear roles to sustain engagement, is finding itself without a usable script. Without a sharp ideological identity or an oppositional tone, Leo resists both praise and critique. He cannot be labeled. He cannot be placed. And because of this, the media has begun to fall silent around him. Not in disapproval, but in confusion.

This silence is not total. Headlines still appear. Profiles are still written. But the rhythm is different. The pope is no longer functioning as a protagonist in a predictable narrative. He is functioning more like a pause in that narrative, a slowing of momentum that refuses to perform the role of either revolutionary or reactionary.

There is something disarming in this. It has left commentators hesitant. Analysts search for patterns, but find only gestures. They expect speeches and instead receive prayers. They wait for confrontation, and encounter stillness. In time, this may lead to a deeper form of attention. Or it may not. But for now, it has created a space rarely seen in the modern coverage of religious life. A space of not knowing.

This kind of interruption is significant. It reveals not only something about the pope, but something about the world that surrounds him. It shows how uncomfortable modern media has become with quiet authority. It shows how deeply the need for narrative has replaced the capacity to witness.

In Leo the Fourteenth, the Church has not chosen someone who will fuel conflict or chase applause. It has chosen someone who absorbs attention without asking for it. Someone who speaks without raising his voice. Someone who renders headlines insufficient.

The modern world tends to associate leadership with mobility. The capacity to shift, to speak quickly, to adapt and respond. But the papacy is not a managerial role. It is not a function of communication or efficiency. It is a form of gravity. A spiritual weight that cannot be accelerated without distortion.

Over time, this understanding has often been obscured. Popes have been measured by action, by visibility, by theological innovation or political influence. Even within the Church, the papal office has sometimes been treated as a platform rather than a presence.

What Pope Leo the Fourteenth is quietly restoring is a sense that the papacy is not defined by momentum. It is defined by density. By the capacity to hold, to carry, to receive and bear what others cannot absorb. His early days have not impressed through activity. They have settled through stillness. They have reintroduced the image of the pope not as an initiator, but as a container of responsibility.

This is not passivity. It is spiritual mass. It is the recognition that the one who sits on the chair of Peter must first sit with the weight of Peter's task. To be responsible not for public clarity, but for unseen coherence. To speak not to generate influence, but to name what must remain true even when unspoken.

This gravity is not rooted in institutional power. It is rooted in interior formation. It is what allows Leo the Fourteenth to resist pressure, to decline distraction, to remain slow in a time of acceleration. It is not that he does not feel the burden of his role. It is that he refuses to outsource it. He does not shed the weight by spreading it into programs. He carries it inwardly, as a sign that holiness is not an event, but a form of endurance.

In this model of the papacy, visibility is not leadership. Silence is not absence. Delay is not evasion. All these become instruments through which the real work of the pope begins — the work of stabilizing the Church not through invention, but through presence.

This kind of papacy is more difficult to measure. It does not resolve debates or announce goals. But it returns the office to its original place within the Church's imagination — not as a node of instruction, but as a locus of gravity. The point around which others can walk without being pulled into orbit.

Leo the Fourteenth may not yet have defined his agenda. But he has already redefined the center. By refusing to react, he has revealed that the most powerful thing a pope can offer is not direction, but depth.

For much of the modern Church, holiness has become a private concept. Often admired but rarely expected. It has been abstracted into theological vocabulary or reduced to sentiment. Public holiness, if it appears at all, is often regarded with suspicion. It is either dismissed as performance or rejected as impossible.

But holiness was never meant to disappear from public life. It was never meant to become invisible. It is not noise, but it is not silence either. It is clarity. A form of human presence marked not by perfection, but by coherence.

What Pope Leo the Fourteenth has begun to reawaken is the memory that holiness is possible. That it can be lived in visible ways. That it does not require grand gestures or supernatural signs. It requires fidelity. It requires depth. It requires the courage to be the same person when no one is watching.

In his public demeanor, his pace, his prayer, and his reluctance to dominate, Leo offers something that transcends image. He does not present himself as holy. But he carries himself as one who lives in the presence of something greater than the world's attention.

This presence cannot be faked. It cannot be manufactured by tone or costume. It must be formed slowly, in hidden places, through long years of listening and surrender. That is what makes it credible. Because it is not claimed. It is revealed.

And it is being revealed now, in the way he walks, in the way he speaks, in the way he prays without drawing the gaze toward himself.

This credibility matters. Because the Church has not only suffered from scandal. It has suffered from the erosion of trust in the possibility of integrity. It has suffered from a leadership culture that knows how to act holy, but rarely invites holiness to carry weight.

Leo does not teach the virtues. He allows them to be seen. He does not speak of humility. He stands with it. And in doing so, he makes space for holiness to be not only admired but imitated.

This is not a return to moralism. It is not the reappearance of clerical exceptionalism. It is something deeper. The recovery of the interior as a legitimate source of authority. Not authority over others, but authority to endure in the name of Christ.

It has been a long time since the world believed that a spiritual figure could be taken seriously without being strategic. But now, in Leo the Fourteenth, holiness is beginning to appear again as something more than private piety. It is beginning to appear again as the core of public witness.

What makes him credible is not that he speaks well.
It is that he seems to pray even when he is silent.
And in that quiet strength, many are seeing not only a pope, but a possibility.
A possibility that holiness may yet become real again

When Time Itself Begins to Shift

There is a form of authority that speaks not only through decisions, but through rhythm. It changes not only what the Church says, but how the Church moves. It reshapes time.

Modern culture has made speed a moral good. To be relevant is to be quick. To lead is to anticipate. To delay is to appear uncertain. In this environment, even the Church has become conditioned by reaction. Meetings follow crises. Statements precede reflection. Action overtakes discernment.

Pope Leo the Fourteenth has not opposed this pace with arguments. He has resisted it with his life. His pace is not rhetorical. It is real. He walks slowly. He answers carefully. He allows space between moments. And through this, he is inviting the Church to recover something it has neglected — the capacity to wait with intention.

Slowness, in this context, is not hesitation. It is depth. It is the refusal to allow urgency to become a substitute for truth. It is the memory that Christian time is not defined by success or speed, but by faithfulness.

This change is already becoming visible. Episcopal appointments are less rushed. Responses to controversy are less immediate. Even public appearances are spaced with more silence, more prayer, more room for the unspoken.

The pace of the papacy is beginning to recalibrate the tempo of the Church.

This is not simply strategic. It is spiritual. Because Christian life has always been ordered not by competition, but by liturgy. Not by reaction, but by season. Not by resolution, but by patience.

To restore that rhythm is to restore the inner coherence of the Church's life. It allows decisions to emerge from prayer, not pressure. It allows communities to grow, not perform. It allows the soul of the Church to breathe.

There will be those who interpret this slowness as weakness. But in the longer tradition of the Church, slowness is often the sign that something deeper is unfolding. It is how monasteries are built. How saints are formed. How history is made without seeking attention.

Leo the Fourteenth has not announced a different calendar. He has introduced a different pace. And in that pace, something ancient is being remembered. Trust cannot be demanded. It cannot be restored by decree. It cannot be programmed into systems or engineered through communication strategies. Trust returns the way seasons change. Gradually. Invisibly. First as silence, then as air.

In the Church, trust has been damaged by scandal, by inconsistency, by performances of authority that were not rooted in credibility. For years, it has been easier to believe in the structure of the Church than in its soul. Easier to speak of doctrine than to experience communion. Many did not leave out of disagreement. They drifted because they could no longer trust the tone in which they were being addressed.

Pope Leo the Fourteenth has not addressed trust directly. He has not published reflections on integrity or institutional transparency. He has done something more difficult. He has made trust possible again by carrying himself as if trust is already real.

He does not speak to control perception. He does not act to recover image. He does not signal. He simply is. And from that quiet coherence, a new climate is forming.

This climate is not yet strong. It is early. But it is visible in the way people are beginning to pray more simply. In how priests are beginning to preach with less fear. In how laypeople speak of the Church again as something that might still be their home.

No initiative has created this change. No campaign has inspired it. It has come from the space that opens when power stops trying to reassure. When it simply abides.

The return of trust is not the same as the return of control. It is not about being reassured that the Church will succeed. It is about remembering that the Church still belongs to something deeper than the instability of its surface. That it can still be true. That it can still be lived from the inside out.

In this way, Leo the Fourteenth is doing something almost invisible. He is replanting the ground that trust needs to grow. Not through argument. Through presence. Through reverence. Through the refusal to force belief.
And because he is not announcing anything, what is growing is real. What is growing is not based on expectation. It is based on recognition.

The Church is moving again.
But it is no longer running.
It is walking.
And in that slower walk, many are discovering
that time is not something to manage.
It is something to dwell in.

There are moments in the life of the Church when change does not arrive through resolution, but through breath. Not through declarations, but through atmosphere. Before anyone names it, people begin to live it. Before anyone defines it, they begin to notice that something interior has softened.

This is what is happening now.

Across the Church, there is a subtle return of clarity. Not in doctrine. That has never left. But in climate. In the way the faithful move through liturgy. In the way silence is received. In the way people speak of the Church, not with enthusiasm or frustration, but with something simpler — something like peace.

It is as if the air has changed. Not dramatically. Not everywhere. But enough to be felt. The edge of fear has receded from some conversations. The need to prove has lifted from some hearts. There is more patience. Less demand.

This is not because there is less suffering. Nor because the world is easier. The world is still divided. Still fragile. Still loud. But the Church, through the quiet posture of its new leader, is beginning to remember a different rhythm.

A rhythm in which reverence is not rare. In which complexity does not cancel clarity. In which authority is not confused with dominance. A rhythm in which the people of God do not react, but dwell. Do not perform, but remain.

They are breathing again.

Not deeply, not triumphantly. But honestly. The way one breathes after a long silence of tension. The way one breathes after remembering that one still can.

This is the beginning of renewal. Not as a movement. Not as a strategy. But as the reappearance of space.

- Space to pray.
- Space to pause.
- Space to believe again without anxiety.
- Space to hope without embarrassment.

What Pope Leo the Fourteenth has offered the Church is not a project. It is a clearing. A clearing in which something new may grow. Or something old may return.

A Church Quiet Enough to Listen

The most important transformations do not begin with conclusions. They begin with questions that are finally allowed to surface. With wounds that are allowed to remain visible. With truths that are no longer spoken too quickly.

If the Church is truly changing now, it is not through renewal that demands attention. It is through the reappearance of a kind of listening. A listening that does not seek to manage outcomes. A listening that waits for God.

Pope Leo XIV has not spoken a new direction into being. He has cleared the noise that kept the Church from hearing itself. He has not declared what will happen. He has made it possible for something real to happen.

The shape of what is coming cannot be drawn. It will not fit into plans or proposals. It will emerge slowly, from the ground of attention. From the rediscovery that the Church is not first an institution. It is a people who remember how to be still before what is holy.

This kind of Church may not be admired by the world. It may not be loud or successful. It may not be quick to respond or eager to speak. But it will be free. Free to be what it was meant to be. Free to grow without noise. Free to serve without drama. Free to forgive without performance.

And most of all, it will be free to listen.

Not just to the world. Not just to itself. But to the one voice that never shouts. The voice that calls in the stillness. The voice that speaks through conscience, through Scripture, through the cry of the poor and the quiet turning of the soul.

That is the voice Pope Leo the Fourteenth seems to be following. And because he is listening to it, the Church is beginning to listen too.

IV - THE SPIRITUAL LOGIC OF LEO XIV

In a world trained to expect persuasion through contest, and clarity through confrontation, the appearance of mercy as a way of thinking can feel like an evasion. But mercy is not the refusal to think. It is a different form of intelligence.

Pope Leo the Fourteenth does not argue. He does not persuade through competition or conviction. He offers no rhetorical defiance. And yet, around him, positions begin to soften. Tensions settle. Questions are no longer shouted. People begin to speak to one another instead of past each other. He has not resolved disagreement. He has changed the air in which disagreement takes place.

This is because mercy, as he lives it, is not an exception to law or a compromise of truth. It is a form of vision. It sees what is true not only in principle, but in process. It does not ignore sin or failure. It refuses to reduce them to verdicts. Mercy does not ask less of the human person. It expects more — more patience, more prayer, more reverence for the mystery of another soul.

The way Leo governs is shaped by this deeper logic. He does not respond to accusation with rebuttal. He does not defend the Church by condemning its critics. He stands still. He remains open. He waits. And in that waiting, something becomes clear: he does not think in categories that divide. He thinks in rhythms that gather.

He does not balance justice and mercy. He does not trade one for the other. He sees that mercy is what allows justice to begin without violence and to end without pride.

This way of thinking is difficult to articulate. It cannot be summarized in policy. It resists being captured in strategy. But it is becoming visible through his choices. In whom he trusts. In whom he listens to. In what he is willing to postpone. In what he does not need to say.

To think with mercy is not to abandon rigor. It is to accept that clarity does not always arrive on demand. It is to believe that truth must be received, not forced. And that the person who seeks it must first be seen, not managed.

Leo does not think with the logic of debate. He thinks with the logic of accompaniment. And from this place, his words do not demand belief. They create space in which belief becomes possible.

The word "conscience" has long been contested. For some, it is a banner of personal freedom, used to challenge external authority. For others, it is a threat to clarity, often blamed for moral confusion. Between these extremes, its true meaning has faded.

Pope Leo the Fourteenth does not speak of conscience often. But when he does, he speaks of it as something quiet and grave. Something not to be claimed, but to be formed. In one of his few personal remarks to new priests, he said, *"Conscience is not what makes us right. It is what keeps us honest."*

This is not a concession to relativism. It is a recovery of responsibility. Leo does not use conscience to weaken doctrine. He uses it to call people inward. Because he understands that what the Church needs now is not stronger alignment. It needs **deeper attention**.

Conscience, in this light, is not an escape from authority. It is the place where authority begins. Not imposed, but received. Not as a voice of impulse, but as the slow unfolding of what must be done — not to be safe, but to be true.

The effect of this reframing is already taking shape. Pastoral conversations are changing. Confessors are speaking less about conditions and more about character. Spiritual directors are returning to questions that begin with silence, not advice. Many are rediscovering the interior life not as a refuge, but as a foundation.

Leo does not tell people what they must think. He invites them to enter the place where thinking becomes prayer. He is not dismantling moral teaching. He is asking what it means to follow Christ from the inside, not from position or affiliation.

This has consequences. It removes the false comfort of labels. It challenges both the right and the left to abandon slogans. It asks something more difficult: that each person seek the light of truth **without shortcuts**, and follow it with humility, not pride.

"The conscience does not speak quickly," he once said.

"But when it speaks clearly, it becomes the beginning of peace."

This is the work Leo has begun. He is not updating theology. He is remembering that the Gospel begins with listening — not to oneself, but to God speaking in the depth of the human soul.

In an age of identity and noise,
he has turned attention toward conscience -
not as escape,
but as the still and serious ground
on which holiness begins.

The Weight of the Wounded

There is a kind of authority that does not come from knowledge, or position, or rhetorical power. It comes from suffering — not as drama, but as endurance. It is not loud. It is not even visible at first. But once it is seen, it cannot be imitated.

Pope Leo the Fourteenth does not speak about his own pain. He does not evoke his years in the barrios of Peru as evidence of understanding. But those who know him say that he listens differently. He does not look away when wounds are named. He does not try to soften grief with explanations. He lets the truth of suffering remain intact.

This is a different kind of strength. It is not the strength of overcoming. It is the strength of staying close.

In his earliest homilies as pope, Leo made no sweeping claims about healing or transformation. He simply said,

"We are entrusted with wounds, not with solutions."

This sentence contains more than pastoral insight. It contains a theology of the cross. Because what gives Leo his weight is not that he knows what to do. It is that he does not flinch before the reality that many things cannot be undone — only carried, only accompanied.

In a world where suffering is often commodified or avoided, this posture feels unfamiliar. It does not promise comfort. It promises fidelity.

This is why many people who have been hurt by the Church are not looking for new programs. They are watching Leo. They are noticing that he does not defend the institution against their pain. He does not ask them to forgive quickly. He does not ask them to come back. He stands still, and he listens.

There is an authority in that stillness. Not because it resolves. But because it refuses to disappear.

To lead with suffering is not to lead with sentiment. It is to recognize that spiritual authority must pass through vulnerability. Not performatively, but quietly, inwardly, until what remains is not persuasion, but presence.

This kind of leadership cannot be marketed. It cannot be systematized. It has no title. But it changes the room. It softens the heart. It builds trust. And it reminds the Church that her greatest strength was never in how she managed pain, but in how she allowed Christ to suffer within her. Leo the Fourteenth carries this truth without explanation. He does not display it. He does not teach it. He lets it shape the way he waits, the way he listens, the way he governs.

"The Church is not here to be strong," he once said.
"She is here to remain with those who are not."

In much of the modern world, truth is expected to arrive quickly. It is measured by immediacy. We ask for statements. We ask for outcomes. We ask for positions that can be repeated, defended, shared, or opposed. In this environment, patience is often mistaken for weakness. Silence is mistaken for uncertainty. Waiting is confused with evasion.

But truth does not always arrive on demand. It does not respond to pressure. It reveals itself through fidelity, not force. And Pope Leo the Fourteenth seems to understand this with unusual depth.

He does not rush to clarify when provoked. He does not answer questions before he has sat with them. His clarity comes slowly, but when it does arrive, it is grounded. It does not react. It endures.

This is not because he avoids decisions. It is because he does not confuse decisiveness with wisdom. For him, clarity is not a style. It is a fruit. A fruit that grows in the silence between instinct and insight.

He once said in a private address to a group of seminary formators,

"Truth that is rushed becomes opinion. Truth that is endured becomes light."

This posture of patience is not passive. It is active waiting. A waiting that allows truth to rise from within conscience, community, and prayer — not just from external demands.

And this is beginning to reshape how others speak and lead around him. Bishops are answering questions with more stillness. Parishes are taking more time in liturgy. Even theological debates are showing signs of slowing down — not because they are resolved, but because the pressure to win them is being replaced by the call to understand what is at stake.

Leo is not giving the Church less certainty. He is reminding it that certainty without patience is fragile. That conviction without reverence becomes noise.

In him, patience is not an absence of courage. It is the presence of interior maturity. It is what makes his judgments more than reactions. It is what gives his teaching a weight that cannot be traced to his volume, only to his silence.

This kind of moral clarity is difficult to teach. It is difficult to measure. But it is immediately recognizable when it appears. Because it is the kind of clarity that stays.

Leo the Fourteenth is not waiting because he
does not know.
He is waiting because he refuses to pretend he
already knows everything.
And in that space, the Church is being invited
to remember that truth, when it is true,
does not need to be hurried.
It needs to be heard.

Simplicity as Witness – How Humility Speaks

There is a language that requires no translation. It does not depend on eloquence or volume. It does not draw attention to itself. It moves quietly through the world and leaves clarity in its wake. This is the language of humility.

Pope Leo the Fourteenth does not present himself as modest. He simply refuses to pretend that the papacy exists to elevate the person who holds it. His daily choices are unremarkable at first glance. He wears what he needs. He walks without display. He speaks as if every sentence must first pass through conscience.

This simplicity is not for show. It is not a message. It is the absence of a message. It is what remains when no one is trying to appear holy, or persuasive, or significant.

And yet, it speaks. It speaks more than words can. It reveals an inner life that is not trying to escape itself. It reveals a man who is not afraid to be seen without control.

"When you do not fear being misunderstood," Leo once said quietly to a group of young priests, "then your words begin to carry meaning."

Simplicity, in this sense, is not aesthetic. It is spiritual discipline. It is the refusal to manipulate the impression one makes. It is the trust that truth, when embodied faithfully, will find its own way to be known.

In a Church that has often been wounded by spectacle, the sight of a leader who does not seek attention is not just refreshing. It is healing. It allows others to breathe. It creates a space where trust can begin to grow again.

This witness is subtle, but contagious. Cardinals who once focused on public image have begun speaking more quietly. Diocesan leaders are paying closer attention to their gestures. The faithful are noticing that the pope does not speak more than necessary, and they are beginning to listen more attentively to what he does say.

This is the power of humility. It does not dominate a room. But it changes the room. Not through force, but through presence.

It says: You do not need to speak to be seen. You do not need to impress to be believed. You do not need to perform to carry meaning.

And that truth is beginning to shape the imagination of the Church once again.

The modern world trains its leaders to be visible. To be known is to be relevant. To be watched is to be trusted. And in this logic, presence becomes performance. Authority becomes the careful management of light and attention.

But Pope Leo the Fourteenth has quietly broken this pattern. He has stepped into the most visible office in the Catholic world and chosen not to fill the frame. He appears without fanfare. He walks without theatre. He speaks, and then he stops. What remains is not his image, but the space his absence has made.

This is not withdrawal. It is clarity. It is the return of a forgotten truth: that power, when it is real, does not need to be seen. And leadership, when it is faithful, does not require affirmation.

"The shepherd is not known by how often he is seen,"
Leo once said.

"He is known by whether the sheep feel watched over when he is not there."
This rejection of spectacle is not an aesthetic preference. It is a theological position. It affirms that presence does not equal grace. That visibility does not guarantee meaning. That the most important things in the life of the Church — holiness, conversion, reconciliation — happen in places the camera will never go.
And the Church is beginning to feel the difference.
Public liturgies are less ornate. Statements are less polished. Faces are more at ease. The demand to be noticed has begun to lift. And in that release, there is room again for reverence.
Spectacle, for all its appeal, exhausts. It trains the heart to seek reaction instead of truth. But Leo's stillness disarms this instinct. He has refused to become the center of every frame. And because of that, the faithful are remembering that the Gospel does not require a spotlight. It requires depth.
Even in Rome, among officials accustomed to planning optics and choreography, the tone is shifting. More silence. Fewer staged encounters. A slower walk. Not to hide. But to remind the

world that the Church's center is not the figure of the pope — it is Christ.

Leo's refusal to dominate the stage is not a sign of detachment. It is a sign of devotion. He is showing the Church how to disappear into the truth it claims to serve.

Living Without Defensiveness

It is rare today to see a public figure who leads without defending himself. Most power structures are held in place by explanation, correction, and the instinct to respond. The more visible the role, the more fragile it becomes. Confidence is often confused with certainty. Silence is treated as weakness. Every statement must be backed by control.

Pope Leo the Fourteenth has broken that rhythm. He does not explain himself. He does not correct misreadings. He does not rush to clarify. And yet, his presence does not feel uncertain. It feels secure.

This is not the security of ego. It is the steadiness of a man who does not need to be protected. A man who knows that truth is not a possession to be defended, but a light that will remain even if misunderstood.

"The truth does not depend on us believing it," he once said quietly.

"It depends on us not fearing it."

This posture is not passivity. It is a form of strength so interior that it cannot be provoked. Leo does not control the conversation. He changes its temperature. He does not withdraw. He remains still. He allows pressure to pass through him rather than reacting to it.

This lack of defensiveness has become one of the most disarming aspects of his papacy. It confuses those who expect argument. It softens those who expect opposition. It has created a space in which disagreement no longer feels like a battle, but like a shared attempt to understand.

The Church has needed this posture for a long time. In the face of scandal, criticism, and confusion, many leaders have instinctively tried to protect the institution. Others have tried to reform it through noise. Leo has chosen neither path. He does not protect the Church. He trusts it. He does not fear critique. He welcomes it. And in doing so, he has begun to heal something deeper than policy. He has begun to heal the fear that lives beneath so much of modern leadership.

This spiritual confidence is not visible at first. It does not announce itself. But its effect is unmistakable. It brings peace. It lowers resistance. It allows the Church to stand not by force, but by depth.

Leo's example is not one of reaction, but of rootedness. He stands because he knows where he stands. And that knowledge, carried in silence, gives others the courage to stop defending themselves and begin listening again.

He does not need to win.
He does not need to control the story.
Because he is not holding the truth like a shield.
He is holding it like a flame.

For too long, much of the Church's public voice has been shaped by fear. Fear of decline. Fear of being misunderstood. Fear of losing cultural ground. Even holiness, which should be the language of freedom, has often been framed in terms of defense — a way to draw borders, to hold a position, to compete for legitimacy in a noisy world.

But holiness is not competitive. It does not need to win. It does not argue for itself. It simply exists — quietly, fruitfully, and with the kind of peace that cannot be imitated.

This is what Pope Leo the Fourteenth seems to carry. His holiness does not declare itself. It does not react. It is not interested in moral posturing. He walks without anxiety. He leads without pressure. He speaks without needing to prove the Church is right.

"The Gospel is not afraid, It has already survived everything that could oppose it."

This is not passivity. It is a refusal to make faith into a contest. It is a decision to let grace speak through coherence, not competition. And it is changing the emotional atmosphere of the Church.

Bishops are stepping back from public performance. Priests are preaching without attack. Laypeople are beginning to speak less in slogans and more in testimony. These are not strategies. They are signs that fear is beginning to recede.

Because when holiness stops competing, the Church begins to breathe.

It no longer tries to mirror the energy of the world. It no longer tries to win cultural arguments through volume. It remembers that it was never called to dominate. It was called to witness. And witness, when it is real, needs no validation.

What Leo is restoring is the dignity of a Church that does not defend its relevance, but trusts its source. A Church that leads not by imposition, but by invitation. A Church that does not need to be seen as right, because it is more concerned with remaining true.

This kind of Church does not threaten. It does not retreat. It stands where Christ stood. With the poor. With the forgotten. With those who have been hurt and who no longer ask to be impressed — only to be loved.

Beyond Strategy – The Return of Mystery

Modern institutions depend on strategy. They plan, forecast, measure, and adapt. In this model, progress is the result of calculation. Even the Church, often reluctantly, has absorbed this logic. It has learned to speak in terms of initiatives, outcomes, alignment, and metrics.

But there is another way of leading. One that does not begin in analysis, but in prayer. One that does not seek to master events, but to serve what is already unfolding through grace. This is the way of mystery.

Pope Leo the Fourteenth has made no major plans. He has published no bold roadmaps for reform. He has not outlined his vision in programs. Instead, he walks slowly. He governs through presence. He leads through patience. And beneath all of this lies his deepest gift: the ability to trust mystery.

"The Church does not need to be efficient, she needs to remain close to what is real."

What is real, in this vision, cannot always be managed. It cannot be mapped in advance. It must be discerned, listened to, allowed to emerge. It must be followed.

This is not an absence of leadership. It is a different kind of attentiveness. A refusal to pretend that the Spirit can be scheduled. A willingness to remain in uncertainty without closing it down too soon.

Mystery is not confusion. It is depth. It is what remains when we stop trying to reduce the Church to what we can understand. It is the silence before decisions. The prayer behind discernment. The reverence for what cannot be explained and yet is most true.

By returning mystery to the center of leadership, Leo is reminding the Church that not every question needs an answer. Not every crisis needs a plan. Not every moment requires a response.

Sometimes, what is needed is to remain still. To keep watch. To wait with God.

This is difficult. It requires humility. It requires the strength to say, we do not know yet. But it also creates the only space where something truly new can emerge — not from invention, but from fidelity.

Catholic moral teaching has always rested on more than rules. At its core, it is a vision of what it means to be human — a vision formed not in the courtroom of ideas, but in the sanctuary of prayer.

But over time, moral language in the Church has often become defensive. It has been used to draw lines, to issue warnings, to settle disputes. In doing so, it has sometimes lost its interior rhythm. It has become separated from wonder.

Pope Leo the Fourteenth does not speak often about morality in the formal sense. Yet his entire papacy is forming a new kind of moral atmosphere. One not built on positions, but on presence. One that does not begin with judgment, but with attention.

"The first duty of conscience is to kneel," he once said.

"From there, the soul begins to see."

This is moral imagination — not as fantasy, but as the capacity to perceive what is good because one has first prayed with it. It is not less demanding than rules. It is more demanding. Because it requires not only knowledge, but reverence.

Leo governs from this place. He does not reduce questions to answers. He returns them to contemplation. He asks those around him to consider not only what is permitted, but what is faithful. Not only what is right, but what is merciful. And not in theory, but in light of God's gaze.

This way of thinking is already changing how some in the Church approach moral complexity. There is more patience. More silence. More willingness to hold tension without needing to resolve it prematurely. There is a growing recognition that moral formation begins not in training, but in prayer.

Because prayer changes the way we see. It breaks open the categories we inherit. It softens the heart without dulling its clarity. It helps the soul recognize what is holy not by argument, but by the gravity of grace.

Leo the Fourteenth does not propose a new moral code. He reminds the Church that ethics without intimacy become empty. That conscience without prayer becomes calculation. That holiness without wonder becomes ideology.

Discernment as Governance

Leadership is often expected to be swift. The world asks for clear answers, immediate direction, measurable outcomes. The Church too has absorbed this habit. It sometimes confuses pastoral care with administrative speed. But discernment is not designed to move quickly. It is not designed to respond. It is designed to reveal.

Pope Leo the Fourteenth has made his way of governing an act of discernment. He does not begin with judgment. He begins with presence. He allows situations to unfold before he names them. He allows time to clarify what urgency often distorts. What may seem slow from the outside is actually a form of deep attention.

This slowness is not indifference. It is justice. Because justice, in the deepest Christian sense, is not simply the correct outcome. It is the right movement of the heart. It is the refusal to decide from fear, or pressure, or appearance. It is the choice to allow every soul, every situation, every question its full weight before action begins.

Leo's form of discernment requires listening that does not rush toward closure. It seeks the full voice of the Spirit, which does not always arrive with certainty. And this listening shapes the kind of governance that allows truth to emerge without force. It creates space in which decision becomes a response to grace, not a reaction to expectation.

This changes the moral tone of leadership. It allows complexity to be carried with care, not resolved with haste. It allows leaders to seek clarity without control. And it allows the Church to act from interior peace, not institutional anxiety.

Such governance is not passive. It is steady. It does not hide behind process. It walks through process with integrity. Because slowness is not a delay in action. It is the discipline by which action becomes worthy of trust.

The result is a leadership that moves without spectacle. That listens without insecurity. That waits not because it is weak, but because it understands that the Church's mission is not to respond to noise, but to remain faithful to the deeper truth unfolding beneath it.

The Church has long been described as both visible and invisible, both structure and mystery. But over time, the visible has often overwhelmed the invisible. Meetings, systems, budgets, and reputation have taken precedence over prayer, presence, and holiness. In many places, the Church has been treated as a machine that must be kept running, rather than a living temple where God is encountered.

Pope Leo the Fourteenth does not speak against institutions. But he does not treat the Church like one. He treats it as something sacred, not because of its size or history, but because of its origin. He moves through it as if it were a sanctuary. He governs it as if its walls were made of people, not concrete. His silence is not administrative. It is liturgical.

This is calling others to return to the interior of the Church. Not the internal politics, but the interior reality. The place where holiness lives. The space where prayer is not preparation for action, but action itself. The depth where doctrine is not a concept but a light.

Under Leo's influence, many are beginning to rediscover the Church not as a vessel of influence, but as a dwelling place. The signs are quiet. Priests lingering longer in silence after Mass. Bishops praying publicly without commentary. Religious orders returning to their founding devotions. These are not reforms. They are reminders.

The Church is not effective when it is efficient. It is faithful when it is reverent. It is fruitful when it is still. The more it becomes a place of inner clarity, the more its actions begin to carry weight. Not because they are louder, but because they are rooted in God.

This is not a return to idealism. It is a restoration of center. The Church is not first a builder of plans, but a house of presence. It exists so that souls may enter into something larger than themselves and still find that they are known. It exists to echo the life of Christ, not in noise, but in form.

What Pope Leo is doing is not dismantling the institution. He is revealing the temple that still lives within it. A temple made of prayer. A temple shaped by silence. A temple that cannot be mapped, only entered.

The Church is not beginning again.
It is remembering what it already is.
And as it does, it is becoming visible again from the inside out.

When Christ Becomes Visible Again

At the heart of the Church is not a message but a person. Not a program but a presence. The Gospel is not a slogan or a rulebook. It is the life of Christ, unfolding again in the life of the Church, whenever she becomes quiet enough to remember who she is.

This is what is beginning to happen now.

Not because of any single decision. Not through sudden change. But through a return to breath. The breath of prayer. The breath of reverence. The breath of a Church that has stopped trying to make itself heard and has begun to listen again.

In this new climate, something more than reform is taking place. Christ is becoming visible again. Not as an idea. Not as an image. But as a way of walking. A way of speaking. A way of remaining with the poor, the quiet, the forgotten. A way of suffering without bitterness. A way of loving without control.

This is not being organized. It is being allowed. It is emerging through the silence Leo the Fourteenth has carried into the center of Catholic life. A silence that does not retreat, but reveals. A silence that does not weaken the Church's voice, but purifies it.

Where this leads cannot be planned. But its direction is already clear. It leads toward simplicity. It leads toward conscience. It leads toward holiness that does not announce itself. It leads toward a Church that does not look inward to protect itself, but opens inward to become transparent.

And through this transparency, Christ begins to appear again.

Not as the subject of discussion. Not as the justification for power. But as the face people encounter when they enter the room. As the stillness in the pope's gaze. As the gentleness in a homily that does not need to impress. As the courage to wait when everyone else demands speed. As the presence that remains when everything else has been explained.

This is not the recovery of an image. It is the recovery of a life. The life of Christ breathing again in the body of his Church. Not loudly. Not suddenly. But unmistakably.

V - NEW WAY OF FOLLOWING

Most models of leadership expect followers to move quickly. A strong voice speaks, and others begin to respond. A decision is made, and those downstream adjust. But the papacy of Leo the Fourteenth is not built on pace. It is built on stillness. And so, those who would follow him cannot follow in motion. They must follow by becoming still themselves.

This kind of imitation does not come naturally. In a world shaped by the speed of reaction, stillness feels like passivity. But stillness is not delay. It is attention. It is the refusal to act from impulse. It is the discipline to remain where God already is, before imagining where he should be next.

To imitate Leo the Fourteenth is not to copy his style. It is to enter the posture that holds his speech, his rhythm, his restraint. It is to become a Church that waits before it teaches, that listens before it plans, that pauses before it builds.

This way of following requires something deeper than loyalty. It requires trust. Trust that what matters most in the life of the Church is not managed from the top, but emerges from the interior lives of her people. That holiness grows not by being pushed, but by being rooted.

A parish that follows Leo does not need a strategy. It needs stillness. A family that follows Leo does not need more spiritual activity. It needs more reverent time. A priest that follows Leo does not need to have every answer. He needs to remain with his people in the silence where grace begins.

There is nothing weak about this way of following. It asks more than energy. It asks presence. And presence, when sustained over time, becomes a form of spiritual strength that no pressure can shake.

This is how the Church will grow now. Not by making herself louder, but by becoming more attentive. Not by asserting herself in every arena, but by being still enough to carry what is sacred.

Trusting Without a Map

Much of the Church has grown accustomed to direction. Policies, timelines, statements, schedules. They give the illusion of certainty, the sense that we know where we are going. But the deeper Christian life has never been a path marked by clarity. It is marked by fidelity. And fidelity often begins where certainty ends.

Pope Leo the Fourteenth has introduced a way of leading that invites the Church to walk without knowing what comes next. He has not explained the future. He has not drawn new maps. He has simply remained faithful in the present. And through that fidelity, a new form of trust is being born.

This trust is not a feeling. It is a decision. It is what happens when a soul stops trying to predict or manage and begins to rest in God's pace instead of its own. It is the refusal to force a story before it has unfolded. It is the patience to live the Gospel before it becomes strategy.

To live without a map is not to wander. It is to walk by light that is interior, not external. It is to follow God not by seeing the road, but by staying near his presence.

This is difficult in a Church that has often measured faithfulness by momentum. But it is necessary. Because holiness does not grow in control. It grows in surrender. It grows in those who stay close to what is true, even when they do not know where it will lead.

This way of trust is not passive. It is active surrender. It makes space for listening. It lowers resistance to grace. It frees the Church from its obsession with relevance and returns her to her vocation: to remain close to Christ, no matter how unclear the path becomes.

For individuals, this means letting go of the need to feel certain before taking the next step. For parishes, it means being more willing to live with questions instead of always seeking answers. For leaders, it means speaking less from solutions and more from presence.

What is being built now cannot be drawn. It cannot be predicted. It must be lived one breath at a time, with hands open and plans loosened. The deepest movements of spiritual life do not happen quickly. They have their own time, their own gravity, their own silence. Growth in faith does not unfold under pressure. It unfolds through stillness. Through rhythm. Through the grace of remaining.

In a Church long shaped by schedules and the need for visible results, slowness can feel like a problem. But it is not a weakness. It is a gift. It is the time frame of truth.

Pope Leo the Fourteenth does not delay because he is unsure. He waits because he believes that spiritual integrity cannot be forced. He does not lead from momentum. He leads from listening. That posture changes not only his actions, but the spiritual climate around them.

Slowness, when practiced as formation, is not apathy. It is reverence. It is the refusal to interrupt the work that grace is doing beneath the surface. It is the trust that what is real does not need to hurry in order to last.

For the Church, this means returning to the sacraments without anxiety. It means rediscovering silence in the Mass. It means not treating spiritual conversation as therapy or instruction, but as accompaniment.

For communities, it means not rushing transitions. For individuals, it means resisting the demand for immediate change. For spiritual directors, it means refusing to manage conversion as if it were progress.

In this atmosphere, patience becomes more than a virtue. It becomes a culture. A way of life that allows depth to appear in its own time. A way of formation that protects what is delicate, what is true, what must unfold slowly or not at all.

This is how depth is born. Not through force. Through fidelity. Through repetition that is not mechanical, but prayerful. Through time that is not measured in achievement, but in surrender.

The Church will not grow by hurrying.
It will grow by learning to stay long enough
for grace to finish what it starts.

The Interior Laity – Prayer Before Participation

Much has been written about the role of the laity in the Church. Their importance has been affirmed, their gifts recognized, their presence welcomed in many areas of pastoral life. But often this attention has come with an expectation of activity. Laypeople are called to participate, to lead, to speak, to organize. Their holiness is measured by visible involvement.

Yet the deepest contribution of the laity may not be action. It may be presence. It may be prayer that is not performance, but interior readiness. A way of being in the world that is not reactive, but attentive. A form of fidelity that begins in silence and returns to silence, even while living fully in the noise of daily life.

This is the form of discipleship Pope Leo the Fourteenth has made credible again. Not a Church of professionals and events, but a Church of souls who carry the weight of faith quietly. The lay vocation is not a role to be filled. It is a life to be lived from the inside out.

When laypeople pray before they speak, listen before they respond, wait before they act, they become the living conscience of the Church. They remind others that faith is not something we use. It is something we are drawn into. Their witness is not spectacular. But it is stable. And in a time of confusion and fatigue, that stability is becoming luminous again.

This way of life requires discipline. It requires turning away from the idea that more effort means more holiness. It requires accepting that prayer is not preparation for participation. It is participation. It is what makes action truthful. It is what makes community coherent. It is what gives the Church her depth.

Interior lay life is not passive. It is generative. It carries the Church through seasons when programs fail and plans dissolve. It holds families in peace when the world shakes. It brings stillness into conversations that have lost their center.

This is not a withdrawal from mission. It is its foundation. The laity are not a supporting structure for Church activity. They are the soil. From their silence comes the fruit that others do not see being planted, but recognize when it is ripe. For many people, the parish is the only face of the Church they will ever meet. It is where they pray, where they grieve, where they search for meaning. And yet many parishes have been shaped more by administration than by mystery. They are busy. They are structured. But often they are not places of stillness.

A different kind of parish is now becoming possible. One that breathes. One that no longer moves from event to event, but from prayer to prayer. One that no longer tries to measure faith by activity, but welcomes the possibility that holiness grows in quiet ways.

This kind of parish is not built first through planning. It is born through attention. It forms where the liturgy is not rushed. Where the sanctuary is not a stage. Where the homily is not a performance. Where the people are not managed but truly known.

A breathing parish creates time between words. It makes space for those who do not yet speak the language of faith but sense that something sacred is being protected there. It carries the weight of community not by multiplying programs, but by offering presence.

This is not about style. It is about depth. A parish that breathes is a place where people are not pressured to change but invited to stay. Where those who are suffering are not fixed but accompanied. Where the Eucharist is not explained but adored. Where silence is not awkward but welcome.

To build this kind of community requires leadership that is willing to lose control. It requires priests who do not fear silence and people who do not demand constant affirmation. It requires the courage to let the Gospel unfold without packaging it in urgency.

The result is not a more efficient Church. It is a more faithful one. A parish that breathes does not seek to impress. It seeks to remain. And in its remaining, people begin to experience something that is increasingly rare in public life. A place that does not react. A place that holds. A place that waits.

Becoming Real Again

Holiness has never needed to be noticed. It does not rely on display. It does not seek an audience. Yet in a world shaped by visibility, even the pursuit of virtue has become performative. Goodness is often staged. Simplicity becomes a style. Prayer becomes a task to complete or share. And holiness becomes a kind of aspiration rather than a lived reality.

But the holiness that the Church is beginning to remember again is something quieter. It does not announce itself. It is not dramatic. It is not impressive. It is simply real.

This holiness is formed slowly in people who do not chase it but dwell in it. It is shaped by daily fidelity, by interior honesty, by patience with one's own limits and those of others. It appears in people who carry pain without bitterness and offer love without seeking attention.

Pope Leo the Fourteenth has not encouraged perfection. He has created a space where holiness can become honest again. Where it no longer feels like a standard to reach but a life to surrender into. Where it is no longer about avoiding fault but about remaining faithful.

This kind of holiness cannot be defined in simple terms. It does not come with clear signs. But it can be felt. It changes the air around a person. It brings steadiness. It brings silence. It makes people trustworthy not because of what they say, but because of how they stay.

The return of this kind of sanctity matters. It reminds the Church that what makes her beautiful is not her power or clarity, but her interior life. Her people do not need to convince the world. They need to become real again. And from that reality, trust and reverence begin to return.

To become holy in this way is not to escape struggle. It is to walk through it without pretension. It is to live with Christ so fully that nothing needs to be added or explained. Just lived. Simply. Fully. With peace.

One of the most difficult things in spiritual life is to stay. Not to begin, not to try, not to prepare — but to remain. To be present when clarity fades. To be faithful when purpose is obscured. To keep showing up when there is nothing to prove and no one to impress.
This is what the Church is being called into now. A kind of fidelity that is not driven by performance. A form of staying that is not measured by visibility or momentum. A way of remaining that simply refuses to leave the place where God is still working.
For a long time, much of the Church's energy has been shaped by movement. Pastoral planning, structural reforms, media strategy. The desire to adapt and respond has sometimes overshadowed the deeper truth — that what changes hearts is not brilliance or novelty, but presence.
Fidelity is the most underestimated form of witness. It is not exciting. It does not draw applause. It rarely produces immediate fruit. But it is the ground on which everything that matters eventually grows.

The Church that stays is not the one that avoids difficulty. It is the one that keeps returning to the same truth with reverence. The one that does not confuse success with faithfulness. The one that knows the Gospel is not a performance but a life slowly shared.

This does not mean avoiding action. It means refusing to act out of anxiety. It means remaining rooted when others are reactive. It means choosing depth when distraction is easier.

To stay is not to stand still. It is to grow quietly in one place. It is to become known. It is to carry others when they cannot walk alone. It is to protect the sacred in a world that moves too quickly to remember what is holy.

This is how the Church will endure. Not by keeping up. Not by explaining herself constantly. But by remaining herself. Simply. Gently. With strength that does not shout and love that does not abandon.

The Church does not know what will come. History does not reveal itself in advance. Programs will rise and fade. Debates will return in new forms. Structures will evolve. But beneath all of this movement, something quieter is already shaping the future. It is the way the Gospel is lived.

Not declared. Not enforced. But lived.

The Gospel lived gently is not weak. It is not hesitant. It is strong in a way the world has forgotten how to see. It refuses to rush. It refuses to dominate. It makes room. It gives time. It listens longer than expected. It stays after others have left.

This is how the Church will grow again. Not by claiming ground but by holding open space. Not by making louder claims but by becoming more trustworthy. Not by controlling time but by waiting in the time that has been given.

Gentleness is not the absence of clarity. It is clarity without violence. It is the truth that invites rather than demands. It is the presence that does not explain everything but somehow makes everything possible again.

The people who will shape the future of the Church are already living this way. They are not known by their plans. They are not trying to fix everything. They are choosing peace over noise, patience over power, prayer over visibility.

They are not waiting for the future to arrive. They are living it quietly, one gesture at a time.

This is what Pope Leo the Fourteenth has begun to restore. Not an institution in motion. A Church that breathes. A people who trust. A Gospel that does not compete, but endures.

There is no map for what is coming. There is no chart that will predict how long it will take. But there is a path. And that path begins in gentleness. It begins in staying close to what is sacred. It begins in refusing to make the Gospel efficient when it was always meant to be patient. This is not a strategy. It is a way of seeing. A way of walking. A way of remaining with Christ as he remains with us.

The Church that waits for God will not be late.
She will be ready.
Because she has learned not only what to
believe.

VI - HE WHO MAKES AMERICA GREAT AGAIN

Every culture tells itself a story about what makes it strong. In the story America has told itself for generations, strength is movement. It is expansion. It is power on the outside and momentum within. But beneath that movement, something deeper has been lost. Not energy. Not capacity. What has been lost is weight.

Not weight as burden. But weight as gravity. The quiet pull of something real. The grounded presence of someone who does not need to perform to be believed.

The desire to be great again is not empty. It is not foolish. It is a longing. A longing for something that once seemed present and now feels scattered. A longing for rootedness. For coherence. For trust that does not shift with the news or tremble under pressure.

This longing is often misnamed. It is wrapped in slogans and shouted in conflict. But its source is not aggression. It is grief. The grief of a people who do not know who to follow, because every voice demands attention and no voice seems to carry truth.

What America desires is not victory. It is direction. Not dominance. But dignity. Not nostalgia. But weight. The weight of a presence that does not change with popularity or vanish under critique. The weight of someone who listens more than he speaks and stands where others perform.

This is why the figure of Leo the Fourteenth is so important. Not because he is American. Not because he intervenes in policy. But because he carries the one thing that no strategy, party, or program has been able to give: interior authority.

He does not pretend. He does not sell. He does not flatter. He does not win. And because of that, something ancient is beginning to stir again. A recognition that greatness is not something declared. It is something lived without needing to be named.

What America misses is not power.
It is presence.
And Leo the Fourteenth is the rare kind of man
who brings weight without spectacle,
and truth without noise.

The Longing Behind the Slogan – A Nation Searching for Weight

Greatness in American imagination often means force. It means success that cannot be questioned, confidence that cannot be interrupted, dominance that silences opposition. It is defined by visibility, scale, and speed. To be great is to win. To expand. To prevail. To become so large that others must take notice.

This vision has been passed through politics, business, culture, even faith. Churches have absorbed it. Leaders have shaped themselves around it. People have grown to expect that authority must look impressive to be real.

But the Gospel tells a different story. It is not the story of ascension, but of descent. Not the story of triumph, but of fidelity. Not power that dominates, but love that refuses to leave. In the Gospel, greatness is not how far one rises, but how deeply one remains present. It is not built on control. It is revealed in mercy. It is not proven through strength. It is embodied through endurance.

Pope Leo the Fourteenth stands entirely outside the cultural logic of greatness. He does not push. He does not position. He does not seek attention. His presence is shaped not by charisma, but by coherence. Not by confidence, but by trust. He carries a form of greatness that cannot be captured in metrics or campaigns.

He is not successful in the ways the world expects. He is not urgent. He is not calculated. He is not concerned with perception. And for that reason, he has begun to expose how fragile the old forms of greatness have become.

The Gospel does not discard greatness. It transfigures it. It returns it to something real. Something that cannot be faked. Something that outlasts popularity. And that is what Leo the Fourteenth offers, not by design, but by who he has chosen to be.

His presence is not an argument against America's desire for greatness. It is a quiet answer to what that desire was trying to ask.

Most leadership is measured by outcomes. Success is often defined by how effectively one defeats opposition, occupies space, or gains influence. Even within the Church, strength has sometimes been shaped by the logic of competition — who convinces, who commands, who defines the direction of the debate.

Pope Leo the Fourteenth has chosen not to play that game. He does not answer provocation with superiority. He does not treat disagreement as a contest. He does not frame his role as one who must outperform or overpower. He leads without conquering. He speaks without rivalry. He governs without needing to win.

This is not indifference. It is maturity. It is the refusal to center the self in a role that was never about personality. It is the decision to remove ego from authority, and in doing so, to allow the Church to breathe again.

His lack of competition has not made him irrelevant. It has made him credible. Because it reveals a deeper strength — a strength not shaped by dominance, but by discipline. Not the kind that resists others, but the kind that remains faithful when it would be easier to prove oneself.

In a culture shaped by debate and division, this is confusing. There is no clear enemy. No visible victory. But that is the point. The Gospel is not a game to be won. It is a presence to be carried. And Leo carries it with the kind of quiet weight that cannot be argued with because it refuses to argue.

His refusal to compete creates space for others to come without fear. It creates space for nuance. For patience. For truth that emerges rather than triumphs. It redefines authority not as a force to submit to, but as a presence to be trusted.

This is not weakness. It is a different kind of power. One that does not defend its territory, but holds its ground without aggression. One that does not interrupt others to be heard, but becomes the silence in which others hear themselves honestly.

This is how the age of winning begins to end. Not by being defeated. But by becoming irrelevant next to the quiet gravity of someone who no longer needs to win to lead.

A new kind of authority is being born

Modern culture is a constant performance. It rewards volume. It demands visibility. It builds reputations on the ability to dominate a moment and leave no space for stillness. In this arena, to be silent is to disappear. To wait is to fall behind. To reflect is to lose control of the story.

Pope Leo the Fourteenth does not step into this arena. He does not raise his voice to compete with the noise. He does not accelerate to keep pace with public expectation. He does not treat attention as a currency. He remains still, not as an escape, but as a deliberate act of resistance.

His stillness is not withdrawal. It is protest without aggression. A refusal to treat the Church like a platform and the papacy like a performance. In a world that seeks immediacy in all things, his quiet pace becomes a disruption. Not because it stops the world, but because it reveals how breathless the world has become.

This stillness is not emptiness. It is presence. It draws attention not by demanding it, but by creating the space in which others realize what has been missing. In that space, the need to explain fades. The need to impress disappears. What remains is something more essential than persuasion. What remains is truth made visible through calm.

For those watching from the outside, this calm may seem like passivity. But for those who begin to enter it, it becomes something else. It becomes a permission to live differently. To stop proving. To stop performing. To return to the quiet interior where conscience can speak again. The arena continues. The world keeps shouting. But in the middle of it stands a man who does not raise his voice. And because he does not shout, he can be heard more clearly than those who do.

His stillness is not the absence of leadership. It is the beginning of a different kind of leadership. One that governs not through reaction, but through gravity. One that invites rather than interrupts. One that allows others to come to rest in a world that does not allow rest.

Much of American culture today is built on irony. Sarcasm has become a form of protection. Cynicism has become a mark of intelligence. To be sincere is to seem naive. To be gentle is to risk being dismissed. The world does not always mock holiness. But it often mocks softness. And so, many learn to mask their convictions behind cleverness or distance.

Pope Leo the Fourteenth does not play that game. He is not self-deprecating to manage discomfort. He is not strategic in his kindness.

He is simply gentle. Without defense. Without irony. Without the need to appear strong by pretending not to care.

This gentleness cannot be mocked because it does not respond. It does not seek validation. It is not afraid to be misunderstood. It does not try to explain itself in the language of strength. It just remains. Calm. Patient. Real.

In a culture trained to deconstruct everything, a leader who refuses to hide behind irony becomes disarming. The jokes fall flat. The criticism sounds tired. Because what they aim to expose is not pretending. There is nothing hollow to reveal. There is only a quiet man, walking slowly, listening carefully, and refusing to turn hardness into a form of authority.

This is what makes his presence disruptive. Not because it offends. But because it leaves no place for clever dismissal. It speaks with the kind of honesty that satire cannot touch. It is so simple that it cannot be reduced. It is so consistent that it cannot be shaken.

The death of irony begins with the return of sincerity. The kind that does not need to be dramatic. The kind that can be mistaken for weakness. But the kind that eventually outlasts every performance because it was never a performance in the first place.

Gentleness is not passive. It is the choice to be human in a system that trains people to be spectators. It is the refusal to protect dignity by attacking someone else's. It is the decision to hold peace when peace makes no sense.

And in the world that Pope Leo the Fourteenth now stands in front of, this gentleness has begun to look like the only thing strong enough to be trusted again.

Mercy has become a public word. It is often used in speeches, campaigns, and social media. But true mercy does not seek attention. It does not ask to be celebrated. It is quiet, slow, often unnoticed. It requires no confirmation. It simply remains close to pain.

Pope Leo the Fourteenth lives this kind of mercy. It does not arrive with slogans. It does not announce itself through gestures meant for the crowd. It appears in the decisions no one sees, in the tone of his presence, in the space he makes for others to breathe. He does not draw attention to his care. He offers it.

In a culture that rewards visibility and force, this kind of mercy is difficult to understand. It does not try to win arguments. It does not perform kindness to prove a point. It simply stays human. It stays attentive. It stays rooted in the reality of suffering without using that suffering to gain moral ground.

This is where Leo's strength becomes clearest. Not in what he changes, but in what he refuses to betray. He refuses to turn people into objects of strategy. He refuses to flatten the complex into the efficient. He refuses to speak about others without seeing them first.

This is not weakness. It is courage in its most human form. The courage to remain tender when harshness is easier. The courage to continue forgiving when the world demands judgment. The courage to be moved without becoming sentimental. The courage to serve without applause.

The world often views mercy as softness. But in reality, it is the discipline to remain honest in the face of pain. To respond to the cry of another without needing that response to be seen. To offer peace without asking for permission. To stay close when others walk away.

This is the mercy Leo carries. It is not a message. It is not a posture. It is his way of being. And through it, the Church is slowly remembering what it means to act not as an institution, but as a person. Not to broadcast goodness, but to quietly become trustworthy again.

Mercy that expects no recognition does not fade.
It becomes the air others learn to breathe again.
Not because it demands change,
but because it holds what is human
when everything else forgets.

The Courage to Burn Without Consuming

Courage is often mistaken for confrontation. The world expects it to show itself through volume, through bold declarations, through resistance that leaves an impression. But there is another kind of courage, one that is not fueled by opposition, but by interior conviction. It does not shout. It does not dominate. But it burns.

Pope Leo the Fourteenth carries this kind of fire. It is not the fire of anger or ambition. It is not the fire that consumes in order to control. It is the fire that refines. That holds. That endures. It burns in silence, not in protest. It is steady. And it lights the space around it without demanding to be seen.

This fire does not seek to win arguments or impose reform. It does not feed on fear or outrage. It feeds on something deeper — the choice to remain faithful even when no one watches. The decision to hold truth when truth costs more than silence. The will to stay awake when others drift into distraction.

In this way, Leo offers a vision of strength that is unfamiliar. It has no sharp edges. It does not flash. It does not threaten. But it does not go out. It remains lit in the quiet discipline of listening. It gives warmth without burning through. It gives clarity without burning away.

Many people look for fire in spectacle. They expect transformation to come through heat and noise. But real transformation often begins in the fire that does not destroy, but sustains. The fire that endures over time because it is not a reaction. It is a way of being.

This is what makes Leo's courage so difficult to imitate. It is not reactive. It is rooted. It does not draw attention to itself, but it reveals everything around it. And in this light, the Church is slowly learning how to be strong again without turning toward force.

To burn without consuming is to lead without harming. It is to guide without controlling. It is to make space for others to come near, without fear that they will be diminished. This is the courage that the world does not understand. And it is the courage that may yet save it.

Much of modern leadership is built around being seen. Visibility has become a form of influence. It has become a measure of relevance. It is not enough to lead. One must be noticed. One must explain. One must constantly remind the world that one is present.

But Pope Leo the Fourteenth does not seek visibility. He does not try to fill the frame. He does not position himself at the center of every moment. He allows the space around him to remain unoccupied. He allows silence to carry meaning. He allows the weight of his presence to be known without announcing itself.

This is not invisibility. It is confidence. It is a form of leadership that does not need to be reinforced by attention. It does not collapse when ignored. It does not respond to every moment of critique. It remains steady. And in that steadiness, something deeper becomes possible.

The return to presence is not a loss of power. It is the return of power to its rightful form. Power that does not dominate. Power that does not manipulate perception. Power that gives space to others and does not need to be central in order to be true.

In this kind of leadership, the emphasis is not on action but on atmosphere. Not on message but on tone. Not on resolution but on patience. Presence does not solve. It accompanies. Presence does not control. It carries. Presence does not need to be followed. It simply remains.

This is the way Leo governs. He does not present himself as the solution. He does not insert himself into every conversation. He trusts that truth, when lived quietly, is stronger than argument. He trusts that fidelity, when consistent, outlasts novelty.

What emerges is a new kind of credibility. One not based on visibility or recognition, but on the subtle weight of a soul who stays close to what matters without forcing it to be seen. That weight is not measurable. But it is felt. It makes room for others to trust without explanation. It allows belief to grow without proof.

This is the kind of presence that can heal. Not by drawing attention, but by creating the space in which others begin to believe again.

Faith That Does Not Flatter – Truth That Does Not Perform

In many places, faith has become a product. It is packaged to comfort. It is shaped to attract. Its sharp edges are softened to keep the attention of those who might otherwise look away. Truth, too, is sometimes adapted. It is made to sound pleasing. It is dressed to be welcomed rather than endured.

Pope Leo the Fourteenth offers something different. His way of speaking does not flatter. His gestures do not perform. He does not try to win over an audience or guide the conversation toward admiration. He speaks with the quiet freedom of someone who no longer fears being ignored.

This is not defiance. It is clarity. It is what happens when truth no longer needs to be justified by applause. When faith does not need to adjust itself to remain visible. When the Gospel does not need to be adapted, only lived with fidelity.

Many people are weary of messages. They are weary of personalities. They are wary of anything that feels too prepared. In this climate, Leo's tone stands out not because it is brilliant, but because it is unguarded. It offers nothing extra. It seeks nothing in return. It is the sound of someone who speaks from prayer, not from strategy.

This is what gives his words their unusual weight. They do not rise and fall with the moment. They do not stretch to meet a trend. They do not depend on how they will be received. They carry what is true even when the truth is difficult. Even when the world is not ready.

Such faith is not easy to imitate. It requires interior honesty. It requires the courage to speak without measuring outcome. It requires a Church that does not sell itself in order to remain heard. A Church that trusts that what is holy will remain true even if no one applauds it.

Leo is helping the Church remember this. Not by explaining it. But by refusing to depart from it. He does not adjust his voice to match the crowd. He does not hide his beliefs behind softened words. He stands quietly in the center of what is real, and lets that be enough.

There are times when nations lose their sense of continuity. The language of beginnings replaces the language of perseverance. Everything must be new. Everything must be rebranded. In such a culture, endurance can look like stagnation. Fidelity can feel like weakness.

But the deepest strength does not lie in novelty. It lies in remaining. Not because nothing changes, but because something unshakable is being protected. Fidelity is not resistance to progress. It is progress that refuses to forget what makes life worth living.

Pope Leo the Fourteenth does not offer greatness through innovation. He offers it through endurance. His posture does not change with pressure. His voice does not shift with response. He does not chase relevance. He remains in the center of what is true and allows the world to turn around him.

This is the kind of fidelity that rebuilds. It gives people something they can trust without having to explain it. It creates space for memory. It creates space for return. It reminds a fragmented culture that consistency is not failure. It is a form of shelter.

The Church, under his guidance, is beginning to reflect this same steadiness. It is no longer trying to react to every external demand. It is learning to be patient again. To be faithful again. To remain close to the sacred even when that closeness brings no reward.

This kind of greatness is not measured by numbers. It is measured by depth. It is not secured through control. It is revealed through witness. It is the greatness of those who do not leave, even when leaving would be easier. The greatness of those who remember, even when the world forgets.

Endurance is not stagnation. It is the shape of conviction when time tries to wear it down. Fidelity is not preservation for its own sake. It is the refusal to exchange what is holy for what is popular.

This is the greatness Leo offers. A greatness that does not expire. A greatness that does not need a platform. A greatness that does not fade because it was never trying to shine. It was only trying to remain.

The Strength of the American People

There is a strength in the American people that cannot be reduced to its politics or headlines. It does not live in institutions. It does not belong to any party or movement. It is quieter than the noise. Deeper than the argument. It lives in the way people carry each other through loss. In how they begin again after failure. In how they still look for meaning even after being disappointed.

This strength does not appear on stages. It appears in kitchens, waiting rooms, hospitals, sidewalks. It appears in the silence of someone staying present for a friend who has run out of words. It appears in the decision to forgive. In the patience to raise children with hope even when the world seems fractured.

It is easy to believe this strength has been lost. But it has not. It has been buried under cynicism, distraction, and performance. But it remains. And in moments of quiet, it begins to rise again. In moments when people choose love without reward. When they choose faith without certainty. When they choose truth even if it costs. This is why Pope Leo the Fourteenth matters in America. Not because he speaks to the surface. But because he lives at the depth where that quiet strength still exists. He does not direct it. He does not claim to restore it. But he honors it. He lives in such a way that reminds people of what they already carry.

The American people do not need to be told how to be strong. They need to be reminded that they already are. Not because of wealth. Not because of power. But because they still know how to care. They still know how to hope. They still know how to love what is real, even when everything else asks them to perform.

This is not a call to greatness. It is a call to memory. And from that memory, something lasting may still begin.

True strength is not what we build in front of others.
It is what we carry when no one is watching.
And in that strength, the future still has room to take root.

The Pope America Never Asked For, But Needs

In a world shaped by media cycles and political signals, it has become difficult to tell what is real. Everything is framed. Every voice is positioned. Every figure is interpreted before they have spoken. Authenticity is broken down and repackaged into something useful for someone else's agenda.

Pope Leo the Fourteenth resists this not through opposition, but through stillness. He does not explain himself. He does not try to shape his image. He gives no easy access to his intentions. And because of that, he becomes something the world no longer knows how to handle.

He cannot be spun.

There is nothing in him that seeks manipulation. He does not speak for effect. He does not move for strategy. His presence is not a tactic. It is simply the shape of a man who lives from within. A man who remains rooted in what is true even when the world wants a narrative instead.

This is what makes him so unsettling to some and so compelling to others. He cannot be used. He cannot be reduced. He does not fit into the categories that the age of reaction depends on. He is too slow to satisfy headlines. Too quiet to excite. Too real to market.

And yet he remains.

He remains at the center of a Church that has long needed to breathe again. He remains at the edge of a world that has forgotten how to trust. He remains not as a symbol of power, but as a witness to something deeper than persuasion. He remains without demanding, without dividing, without performing.

This is not the pope the world asked for. But it may be the one it needs. Not because he solves anything quickly. But because he refuses to become another figure of control. He is the opposite of a spectacle. And in that quiet reversal, he becomes a doorway.

A doorway back to conscience. A doorway back to depth. A doorway back to the truth that does not need to win in order to endure.

But this is not only about him.

It is about the kind of world that can still recognize truth when it is not marketed. The kind of culture that is tired of spectacle and ready for sincerity. The kind of people who no longer want to be entertained, but want to be grounded. People who are quietly waiting for someone who will not demand, will not flatter, will not sell them anything — only remind them of who they are when they are most awake.

Leo the Fourteenth is not here to create a movement. He is not trying to become a symbol. That is why he can become a mirror. A mirror for what is missing. A mirror for what still matters. A mirror for the quiet strength of those who have not given up but who no longer know where to place their trust.

And slowly, without design, that trust is beginning to return. Not to institutions. Not to language. But to the presence of someone who simply remains. And in that remaining, makes space for others to stop spinning too.

This is how renewal begins. Not through noise. Not through strategy. But through the reappearance of what cannot be distorted. Through lives that no longer perform. Through words that no longer shift. Through faith that no longer needs to explain itself to remain true.

When truth no longer needs to be managed,
when trust no longer needs to be manufactured,
a deeper kind of strength becomes possible.
Not the strength to rule,
but the strength to remain.

VII - THE COST OF BEING REAL

There is a kind of heaviness that does not come from conflict or failure. It comes from holding something whole in a world that rewards fragments. From refusing to adjust truth to fit expectation. From remaining one's full self when it would be easier to become smaller, softer, safer.

Pope Leo the Fourteenth carries this kind of weight. It is not a burden he seeks. It is a consequence of living without disguise. Because when a person stops managing how they are seen, when they stop reacting to every voice and simply remain, the silence around them becomes sharp. It draws attention. It invites misunderstanding. And it begins to press inward.

This is the weight of integrity. It does not make someone rigid. It makes them steady. But it costs. It costs ease. It costs approval. It costs the quiet comfort of being understood by the world without having to explain anything.

Leo does not signal. He does not posture. He does not smooth out the sharp corners of what he believes to make it more acceptable. And for that reason, he often walks alone. Not in isolation, but in clarity. A clarity that others admire but do not always join.

There are easier ways to lead. There are quicker ways to win trust. There are simpler paths to influence. But Leo has chosen the path where nothing is earned cheaply. Where each word must match the interior life it rises from. Where each gesture is not allowed to become performance. Where the soul must remain whole, even when the world prefers illusion.

This is not a heroic story. It is not a tragedy. It is the quiet weight of someone who has chosen to remain real in a world that asks for roles. And that weight does not break him. But it leaves a mark.

In most forms of leadership, clarity is managed. Messages are shaped to guide perception. Silence is avoided because it invites interpretation. To lead, in this model, is to explain constantly, to control reaction, to eliminate confusion before it forms.

Pope Leo the Fourteenth has taken a different path. He does not defend himself. He does not clarify what others misread. He does not intervene when his stillness is interpreted as absence. He allows himself to be misunderstood. Not carelessly, but deliberately.

This is not a rejection of truth. It is a recognition of what real clarity demands. It demands the courage to let others carry their own questions. It demands the strength to let perception remain incomplete. It demands trust in something deeper than public agreement.

To be misunderstood without correcting it is one of the quietest forms of suffering. It isolates. It strips away the comfort of being seen as good. It reveals how much we rely on being praised in order to remain steady. And it slowly teaches that peace does not come from being known. It comes from being faithful.

Leo's posture is not mysterious. It is simply unguarded. He lives as he prays. He leads as he listens. And that coherence often confuses a world that expects more performance, more strategy, more anticipation of reaction.

But the price of that confusion is high. Misreading becomes a kind of shadow he must carry. His stillness is called indecision. His slowness is seen as passivity. His mercy is taken as weakness. His silence is labeled avoidance. He does not correct any of it. He lets it stand. And in that standing, something begins to shift.

His refusal to shape the story gives the story space to breathe. It invites others to look again. It allows time to become the interpreter. And in that space, the meaning begins to deepen.

Pope Leo the Fourteenth does not move at that pace. He speaks slowly. He decides with care. He allows time to open. And in doing so, he steps outside the rhythm of what most people expect from leadership. He is not slower because he is uncertain. He is slower because he refuses to be rushed by fear.

But slowness comes at a cost. Those who move slowly in a world built on speed will often find themselves walking alone. Others move ahead. Conversations shift without waiting. Decisions are made before questions finish forming. And in that space, the one who remains unhurried begins to feel the distance grow.

This loneliness is not dramatic. It is quiet. It shows up in subtle ways. A sense of being slightly out of sync. A realization that others have already turned the page. A calm knowing that trust will take longer to form because it cannot be accelerated.

Leo carries this distance without resentment. But it is real. To remain unhurried in a system shaped by urgency is to choose a kind of separation. Not because of superiority, but because of rhythm. Because waiting has become its own form of resistance.

There are moments when this isolation deepens. When the world misreads silence as absence. When the choice to pause is mistaken for fear. When those who walk faster assume they lead more clearly. In these moments, the temptation is not to change the path. It is to change the pace. To hurry just enough to be re-included. To speak just enough to be noticed.

Leo does not give in to that temptation. He stays with the rhythm he knows to be true. And in doing so, he walks with God at a pace that is no longer common. A pace that allows for depth. A pace that does not demand resolution. A pace that creates space for others to slow down, too.

The Temptation to Soften

To be true is not only to speak clearly. It is to remain consistent when that clarity begins to cost something. And eventually, it always does. Truth, when lived without disguise, meets resistance. It slows things down. It unsettles the rhythm of comfort. It demands patience from those who would rather move on.

In these moments, the temptation is not to abandon the truth. It is to soften it. Just enough to be accepted. Just enough to keep the peace. Just enough to stay included without feeling compromised.

Pope Leo the Fourteenth knows this temptation. He does not meet it with defiance. He meets it with silence. Not because he has nothing to say, but because he refuses to change his tone to make truth easier to receive.

There is a cost to this refusal. He is not celebrated by everyone. He is not followed with the energy that charisma often produces. He is not quoted for dramatic effect. His words do not rise in tempo. His presence does not shift with the mood of the world. He simply remains. And that remaining becomes its own quiet answer to the temptation to soften.

To soften truth is not always to lie. Often, it is to remove just enough of its sharpness so that it fits more easily into the moment. But truth that has been trimmed for comfort loses something essential. It becomes something remembered rather than something that changes people.

Leo has chosen to preserve that edge. Not by being harsh. But by being whole. He refuses to reduce the Gospel to something more agreeable. He refuses to speak about conscience in language that removes responsibility. He refuses to speak about mercy in language that removes truth.

And because of that, he stands in a space that can feel narrow. But it is the space that protects integrity. It is the space that allows the soul to remain unbroken. It is the space that makes real change possible — because it comes from a voice that has not negotiated itself away.

There are moments when silence becomes more than stillness. It becomes absence. Not the absence of God. But the absence of echo. The absence of reaction. The absence of visible movement in response to what is offered with care.

For leaders who live from integrity, this is often the hardest space to remain in. Not the space of opposition. But the space where everything is quiet. Where there is no immediate confirmation that the path is right. Where the voice goes out and nothing seems to return.

Pope Leo the Fourteenth does not resist this silence. He walks into it. He does not demand recognition or results. He does not measure his presence by its visible effect. He allows his fidelity to fall into emptiness if it must. Not because it is meaningless. But because he trusts that meaning does not always arrive with affirmation.

To remain faithful when nothing responds is to practice a deeper kind of listening. A listening that expects nothing in return. A listening that continues even when all signs suggest stopping. It is not performance. It is not waiting for applause. It is the quiet discipline of continuing to be present when there is no signal that anyone remains on the other side.

This silence is heavy. It stretches time. It slows the heart. It can make even the most grounded soul wonder whether anything is changing. But this is the place where integrity becomes more than intention. It becomes form. It becomes the shape of a life that is true, even when no one is watching.

Leo does not fight the silence. He receives it. He lets it pass through him. He lets it become the background in which a different kind of faith can take root. Not faith in outcome. But faith in presence. In the act of continuing when all response has gone quiet.

There is a kind of resistance that does not raise its voice. It does not rally support. It does not respond in kind. It simply refuses to become what it does not believe in. And in that refusal, it begins to reshape the space around it.

Pope Leo the Fourteenth practices this kind of resistance. He does not call attention to it. He does not declare opposition. He does not explain his distance from the language of conflict. He simply does not enter it. He remains still where others perform. He listens where others manage. He waits where others rush to dominate.

This quietness is not passive. It is precise. It is the choice to stand where dignity is preserved, even when that choice goes unnoticed. It is a kind of defiance that does not break the rules, but makes them irrelevant. It removes the need to win. It lets truth remain untouched by spectacle.

To resist without sound is not to disappear. It is to disrupt without spectacle. It creates confusion in systems built on performance. It creates room in conversations shaped by competition. It introduces a rhythm the world does not know how to match.

This is the kind of presence Leo carries. It does not attack. It does not retreat. It simply holds its form. And that holding becomes a sign that another way is possible. A way of being in the world without being consumed by it. A way of leading without taking.

Many expect resistance to be visible. But the most enduring resistance often looks like endurance. The refusal to be hurried. The refusal to explain. The refusal to shout. The refusal to become the very noise one hopes to heal.

The Grace of Invisibility

To disappear from attention is often treated as a failure. Modern leadership expects presence to be measurable, consistent, framed in light. To go unseen is to be considered irrelevant. But invisibility, when chosen or quietly accepted, can become a grace.

Pope Leo the Fourteenth does not seek invisibility, but he allows it. He does not rush to fill the stage. He does not reclaim the spotlight when it moves. He does not insist that his voice remain the center. And in doing so, he begins to reflect something rare — a leader who is not afraid to fade.

This fading is not a sign of weakness. It is strength without reference to self. It is the quiet courage to become small so that something larger can be seen more clearly. It is the willingness to be forgotten in the moment so that the truth remains beyond it.

Invisibility creates freedom. It removes the pressure to perform. It quiets the noise of reputation. It returns the soul to its source. When no one is watching, action becomes honest.

When no one is praising, prayer becomes real. When nothing needs to be managed, fidelity becomes simple again.

Leo accepts this with the kind of clarity that does not need reward. He is not here to be remembered. He is here to be faithful. And because of that, his presence lingers in places where others have passed through loudly but left nothing lasting.

This kind of grace cannot be designed. It cannot be practiced. It comes only when a life is given over fully, when attention no longer defines value, and when the desire to serve is stronger than the desire to be seen.

To be invisible is not to vanish.
It is to make room
for something deeper to remain
without being framed in the shape of the one
who carried it.

Most leadership is tied to results. Influence is measured by movement. Progress is defined by change. To lead without visible outcome is often seen as failure, or at best, irrelevance. But there is another kind of leadership. One that does not rely on momentum, but on depth. One that does not depend on being seen, but on being rooted.

Pope Leo the Fourteenth leads this way. He does not track responses. He does not press for validation. He moves without chasing confirmation. His vision is not shaped by its reception. It is shaped by faithfulness to what must be done, whether or not it is noticed, understood, or completed in his lifetime.

This is not resignation. It is clarity. It is the refusal to reduce vocation to result. It is the quiet courage to plant seeds that will grow in silence, perhaps in another generation, perhaps without name or recognition.

To lead without outcome is not to act without care. It is to act without control. It is to speak truth knowing it may be forgotten. It is to choose mercy knowing it may be dismissed. It is to guide others not toward measurable goals, but toward freedom — even if they walk away unchanged.

Leo's strength lies in this discipline. He does not need to witness the harvest to remain faithful in the planting. He does not need applause to continue the work. His leadership is not transactional. It is not shaped by reaction. It is shaped by integrity that does not depend on impact to remain intact.

This is the kind of leadership that leaves a mark without leaving a trail. It forms those around it slowly. It creates silence instead of spectacle. It makes space instead of demands. And in that space, something more lasting is allowed to take root.

In the end, what remains is not always what was said. Not always what was built. Not always what was seen. What remains is the silence that shaped those things — the silence that held the choices, absorbed the costs, carried the weight without needing to announce it.

Pope Leo the Fourteenth lives from this silence. It is not absence. It is not emptiness. It is the space that makes fidelity possible. It is the ground beneath his restraint. It is the atmosphere around his decisions. It is the condition in which he listens before he acts and waits before he speaks.

This silence is not passive. It holds sorrow. It carries memory. It bears the tension of not knowing when or whether something will change. It receives misunderstanding. It allows the work to remain pure when the world looks away.

And yet, it is also where clarity lives. The clarity that does not depend on speed or praise. The clarity that comes from not needing to prove, to defend, or to explain. It is the silence of someone who has given up nothing essential, even when so much has fallen away.

What remains, finally, is not influence or control. What remains is presence. The presence of a man who has not adapted to survive, but who has remained real in order to serve. A man whose silence does not hide truth, but protects it. A man whose stillness is not delay, but devotion. This silence cannot be taught. It must be lived. It must be waited through. And those who remain with it long enough begin to understand that it is not what happens in public that holds a soul together. It is what remains unshaken when the world no longer responds.

The cost of being real is silence.
And sometimes, silence is the clearest form of truth.
It does not fade.
It does not shout.
It simply remains.

VIII - THE WORLD THAT MIGHT STILL WAKE UP

There are moments in history when the world begins to show signs of exhaustion. Not because it has failed, but because it has been running too long on things that do not last. Image, pressure, growth without depth. These forces do not break the world. They thin it. They leave it breathless.
We are living in such a moment. Everything speaks. Everything demands. Everything moves faster than the soul can follow. The result is not collapse. It is confusion. A loss of orientation. A weariness so quiet that even hope begins to sound like noise.
In this atmosphere, what most people crave cannot be found in new systems. What they crave is something more ancient. Something that does not need to be explained. They want to know what can still be trusted. They want to know who will still be here when the noise fades. They want to know if there is anything left in public life that is not performing.
Pope Leo the Fourteenth does not answer these questions with arguments. He does not offer new rhetoric. He walks through this tired world with something older. A small flame. It does not flash. It does not command. But it remains lit. And the longer it remains, the more visible it becomes.

This flame is not made of ideology. It is not held by power. It is not maintained by approval. It is the flame of a man who has not adjusted himself to stay relevant. A man who does not speak to keep attention. A man who does not move to secure his image. It is the flame of integrity, carried quietly through a world that has begun to forget what real strength looks like.

There is no program that can make a world like this wake up. But there is something in the sight of that flame — carried without explanation, without apology, without collapse — that begins to stir the memory of what was once sacred. And what might still be again.

The Tired World and the Quiet Flame

Every institution begins with purpose. Not with structure, but with vision. Something sacred rises and must be protected. So forms are created. Processes are built. Memory is organized into law. And for a while, the institution carries its soul with integrity.

But over time, forms harden. Processes multiply. Memory becomes language rather than presence. The institution begins to speak about itself more than about the thing it was built to serve. Slowly, the reason for its existence becomes background. What remains is machinery, often well managed, but strangely hollow.

This is how forgetting begins. Not with denial. But with drift.

The Church knows this pattern. Nations know it too. The moment that survival becomes more important than truth, something essential begins to disappear. Language continues. Rituals continue. But the interior fire grows faint. And when people begin to leave, the first reaction is often to adjust the exterior. To reorganize, rebrand, reframe.

But the answer is not in appearances. It is in memory. Institutions do not come back to life by looking better. They come back to life by remembering why they exist.

Pope Leo the Fourteenth does not speak much about reform. He does not change the frame. He changes the center. He reminds the Church that its weight does not come from its history or structure. It comes from remaining close to Christ.

This memory cannot be scheduled. It must be embodied. It must be carried by someone who refuses to manage what was meant to be lived. Someone who does not fear becoming smaller in order to become true.

This is how institutions begin to wake up. Not by expanding. But by remembering. Not by convincing. But by returning. Not by strength. But by truth that is no longer used, only served.

Noise has become the atmosphere of modern life. Not just sound, but the constant demand to react. To be current. To be seen. To speak. It is difficult to remain rooted in a world that does not pause. And in this environment, memory becomes fragile.

Memory is not nostalgia. It is not a return to the past. It is the ability to carry what matters into the present without needing to explain it. Memory is what prevents a soul from being shaped entirely by reaction. It is the soil in which truth remains even when clarity is lost.

Most cultures, when overwhelmed by noise, begin to lose their memory. Not all at once. But quietly. Depth is replaced by motion. Inheritance is replaced by novelty. Wisdom is reduced to content. And those who still remember are often overlooked.

Pope Leo the Fourteenth does not speak often of memory. But everything he does is shaped by it. He moves slowly because he remembers what rush has done to the soul. He governs simply because he remembers what complexity has done to trust. He speaks carefully because he remembers that clarity is not volume.

His presence is a form of memory. It does not compete. It does not adjust. It simply remains. And in that remaining, something returns that the world did not know it had forgotten. A way of being that does not require explanation. A kind of goodness that does not demand recognition. A truth that does not shout to be heard.

This is the memory that survives noise. Not because it is loud enough to win. But because it is quiet enough to last. It becomes a rhythm. A temperature. A tone that begins to heal by making something real feel possible again.

A Church that remembers why it exists
no longer needs to protect itself.
It only needs to remain open
to the presence that gives it life.

The Kind of People Who Do Not Leave

Every age produces a certain kind of faith. In times of triumph, faith is confident. In times of fear, it becomes defensive. In times of confusion, it often disappears.

But in every time, there are some who stay.

They are not louder than the moment. They are not famous. They do not create movements or claim authority. They simply remain. They remain when things are unclear. They remain when they are disappointed. They remain not because they are blind, but because they see something others have forgotten.

These are the people who do not leave. They show up quietly, pray steadily, forgive often, and keep the door open even when no one walks through it. Their lives are not marked by drama, but by coherence. They do not need attention to stay faithful.

The Church survives through these people.

They are not always noticed. But they are there. Lighting candles. Returning to the same pew. Bringing their silence into the liturgy. Carrying their grief into the sacraments. Listening when no one else is listening. Trusting when trust has become costly.

Pope Leo the Fourteenth walks with this kind of faith. His presence gives space for these people to breathe again. To realize that their quiet fidelity was never small. It was never naive. It was never wasted. It was the form of faith the Church was always meant to carry.

The world often celebrates those who leave with courage. And sometimes leaving is honest. But not always. Sometimes leaving is easy. Sometimes it is noise. And sometimes it becomes a way to escape the hard work of remaining close to something that is wounded but still true.

To stay does not mean to accept everything. It means to believe that something deeper is still present. That Christ has not left. That the Church is not a performance but a presence. That holiness does not grow through force but through fidelity.

These are the kind of people who will carry the Church into whatever comes next. Not because they are perfect. But because they did not leave.

Reverence has become rare. Not because people have stopped caring, but because they have stopped pausing. Reverence is not only a posture. It is a rhythm. A way of seeing that does not rush past the sacred. A way of listening that does not expect control.

In the speed of modern life, reverence often looks unnecessary. It slows things down. It does not explain itself. It creates space without using it. And so, it has faded from many rooms — even from some places where it once belonged.

But under Pope Leo the Fourteenth, something is returning. The reappearance of reverence is not dramatic. It is not imposed. It is not even always noticed at first. It shows up in silence that is not awkward. In gestures that are not exaggerated. In words that do not fill every space, but open it.

It appears where people begin to breathe again in the presence of something they do not need to understand in order to trust. It appears where the sacred is not handled, but honored. Where the mystery of God is not managed, but received.

Reverence does not entertain. It does not flatter. It does not perform. And that is why its return is healing. Because it restores the distance that allows love to remain love. It restores the atmosphere in which truth is not pressed into argument but allowed to rest in its full weight.

Leo carries this atmosphere without naming it. He does not teach reverence. He simply does not remove it. And because he does not remove it, others begin to feel its shape again.

In this atmosphere, the Church becomes believable not because of how she speaks, but because of how she stands. Not because of what she says, but because of what she protects without touching. Reverence changes the room. Without instruction. Without force. Just by remaining.

A New Vocabulary of Trust

Trust has become difficult to build and easy to lose. In public life, most words are weighed not by meaning, but by effect. People listen to decide whether to believe, not to understand. And so trust breaks. Slowly. Quietly. Until the most common reaction to anything that claims to be true is hesitation.

What breaks trust is not disagreement. It is inconsistency. It is words that do not match tone. Presence that does not match promise. A Church that speaks of mercy while rushing to judgment. A world that speaks of dignity while rewarding performance.

Pope Leo the Fourteenth does not fix this with messaging. He does not offer better explanations. He speaks less, and from somewhere deeper. His words are not many, but they are steady. He does not adjust their weight to win attention. He does not use language to direct response. He speaks from clarity, not from calculation.

This is where a new vocabulary of trust begins. Not with better phrasing, but with less performance. With speech that does not pressure. With tone that matches truth. With the courage to say less when less is more faithful.

In this vocabulary, trust is not argued for. It is allowed to grow. It takes time. It takes consistency. It takes presence that does not shift under pressure. It takes silence that does not feel like absence.

Leo's language does not compete. It does not seek efficiency. It makes space for the sacred. And in that space, others begin to listen not because they are persuaded, but because they sense something honest. Something that does not rise and fall with strategy. Something that has been lived before it has been said.

Holiness is not a posture. It is not a role. It is not a signal of virtue or a way to be noticed. It is the shape of a life that no longer needs to impress. A life that has come so close to the presence of God that it becomes simple again.

In a world shaped by presentation, this kind of holiness is hard to recognize. It does not stand out. It does not signal anything. It does not want to be seen. And because of that, it becomes the kind of presence others begin to trust without knowing why.

Pope Leo the Fourteenth carries this kind of holiness. Not as authority. Not as image. But as peace. He does not offer himself as an example. He does not speak of holiness often. He simply moves in a way that makes holiness feel possible again — not because it is perfect, but because it is coherent.

This coherence does not draw attention. It removes the need for it. It becomes a form of clarity that leaves no mark except silence. It makes no demands. It expects no recognition. But it changes the atmosphere by making the sacred feel less distant.

True holiness does not ask to be followed. It does not persuade. It simply remains where others rush past. It listens longer. It forgets itself. And by doing so, it allows others to remember who they are before they began trying to become someone else.

This is the kind of holiness that heals. Not through effort. Not through purity of doctrine or scale of effort. But through a quiet that refuses to turn itself into an object. A quiet that reflects the love of God without naming it. A quiet that remains true even when it is invisible.

Nations can do many things. They can build, defend, organize, reform. They can create laws, systems, markets, and movements. They can enforce justice and extend mercy through institutions. But there are some things they cannot make.

- They cannot manufacture meaning.
- They cannot legislate reverence.
- They cannot produce holiness.
- They cannot create memory.

These things do not begin with programs. They begin with persons. With presence. With quiet acts of fidelity that do not need to be seen. They grow in silence, and they hold their form because they are not created for display.

Pope Leo the Fourteenth has not tried to change America. But he has revealed something about its longing. His quiet life, his steady voice, his refusal to perform — all of it uncovers a truth that has nothing to do with politics and everything to do with the soul.

He reminds us that there are virtues no structure can deliver. That there is strength deeper than control. That there is trust beyond messaging. That there is sacredness that can only be received, not managed.

A nation may have resources, freedom, and power. But without reverence, it forgets what those gifts are for. Without silence, it forgets how to listen. Without conscience, it forgets what kind of future is worth protecting. These cannot be imposed. They must be lived into.

Leo brings no answers to these questions. But he holds their weight. Not by diagnosing culture, but by refusing to leave the center of what is still true. And in that quiet refusal, a mirror appears — not to judge, but to reveal.

The Beginning That Has Already Begun

The future is often imagined as something to be shaped. Something to predict, organize, and control. Leaders are asked to provide vision. Institutions are expected to anticipate what comes next. Culture demands a sense of direction, even if it is only for comfort.

But there are moments in history when the future stops responding to plans. Not because it is lost, but because it is no longer willing to be managed. It becomes quiet. It waits. It moves below the surface of things, beyond what strategy can reach.

This is such a moment.

Pope Leo the Fourteenth does not pretend to shape the future. He does not speak in terms of programs or goals. He does not offer a narrative to carry the Church forward. He remains in the present. And in that present, something begins to shift.

The future that matters now will not be built by force. It will not come from brilliance. It will not emerge from speed. It will come from the quiet renewal of conscience. From the slow return of trust. From the patience to let something sacred unfold at its own pace.

This future cannot be planned. But it can be prepared for.

It will rise through ordinary fidelity. Through people who listen. Through decisions that do not adjust truth for acceptance. Through parishes that do not compete. Through friendships that do not perform. Through silence that teaches us how to speak again.

Leo leads without pointing ahead. He does not define what comes next. He only makes space for it. And that space is not empty. It is full of clarity, full of memory, full of peace strong enough to carry what is coming.

Most beginnings do not feel like beginnings. They arrive without announcement. They move quietly. They begin in silence, in stillness, in the small shift of how someone listens, how someone remains, how someone refuses to leave what is true even when it no longer seems visible.

The world may not yet look changed. The Church may still carry the weight of its confusion. The nation may still search for meaning in places that cannot give it. But something has begun. Not through events, but through lives. Not through movements, but through presence.

It has begun wherever someone has chosen not to hurry. Wherever someone has decided not to perform. Wherever someone has stepped back from the noise to hold what is sacred without fear of being forgotten.

It has begun in the quiet of Pope Leo the Fourteenth. In his refusal to answer questions the wrong way. In his gentleness that cannot be spun. In his stillness that does not abandon truth, but holds it open for others to return.

It has begun in the parish that prays without needing to entertain. In the friendship that lasts without needing to prove itself. In the silence that feels like home instead of absence. In the conscience that does not shift with approval.

This beginning cannot be captured. It cannot be accelerated. But it is here. Already. In the slowness that now feels like peace. In the fidelity that now feels like strength. In the Church that is learning again how to be herself.

There is nothing left to predict.
Only something to remain close to.
And in that closeness,
the world that might still wake up
has already begun to open its eyes.

AFTERWORD

This book did not begin as a biography. It did not begin as an argument. It began as an act of attention.

Pope Leo the Fourteenth did not enter public life with a platform or plan. He did not seek the spotlight. He did not fight for position. And when the papacy came to him, he received it not as a victory, but as a burden to carry slowly and faithfully.

What followed was not dramatic. It was not easy to explain. But something began to shift.

He did not speak often. He did not correct the noise. He did not demand clarity from others. He stood at the center of the Church — not as a symbol, not as a performer, but as a witness. A witness to something older than strategy. A presence more trustworthy than posture. A stillness that held meaning without needing to display it.

This stillness became the key.

Through his presence, the Church began to slow. Through his silence, the atmosphere of leadership changed. Through his refusal to compete, trust began to return in places where it had disappeared. And through his fidelity, something almost forgotten came into view again — not as doctrine, not as message, but as life.

This book has followed that life — not to define it, but to dwell near it. It has watched how one man's refusal to adapt opened the way for others to remember. How his willingness to remain real became a quiet mirror for the Church, the nation, and the restless conscience of modern life.

Along the way, we have not made claims. We have not tried to persuade. We have paused. We have listened. And in that listening, the shape of Leo's witness has become clear.

He is not a man of many words. He is not the kind of leader the world expected. He is not solving problems through pressure. He is not competing for attention. He is carrying something instead. And that something has become the quiet flame around which many are slowly beginning to gather.

This is not a movement. It is not a revival. It is not a moment in history to be remembered later with fanfare. It is something slower. Smaller. Stronger.

- It is the return of moral gravity.
- The rediscovery of reverence.
- The recovery of simplicity.
- The reappearance of trust.

And all of it, quietly, through the life of a man who decided not to speak louder, but to speak more truthfully. Who decided not to move faster, but to remain more faithfully. Who decided that the Church did not need to be managed. She needed to be trusted again — to become herself, not through reinvention, but through remembrance.

This book has tried to name that remembrance. It has tried to walk near it without forcing meaning into clarity. It has tried to honor what is being offered without dressing it in words it does not need.

Now the pages fall silent. The flame continues. And whatever the future brings, it will be shaped — not by this text, not by headlines, not by plans — but by the same stillness we now understand more clearly than before.

Not because it explained itself.
But because it never left.

And so we walk away from these pages not filled, but opened.

Not instructed, but steadied.

Not certain of the future, but less afraid to live in its silence.

If there is anything Leo the Fourteenth has taught without saying, it is this: that truth does not need to be forced. That faith does not need to be visible. That greatness does not need to arrive.

It is already here — in the gentleness that does not break, in the conscience that does not shift, in the quiet that refuses to perform.

These are the foundations we had forgotten.
And now, through one man's fidelity, they have returned to the surface. Ready to be trusted again. Ready to be carried. Ready to begin.
Without urgency.
Without applause.
Without fear.
Only with presence.
And from that presence, everything that matters may begin to live again.

S.T.REED

***

SOURCES AND REFERENCES

This list contains the primary sources, inspirations, and reference points used or evoked in the writing of the book 'Pope of Hope – The Man Who Will Truly Make America Great Again'. While the book is a contemplative and interpretive work rather than an academic text, the following materials helped inform its tone, structure, and theological imagination:
The Catechism of the Catholic Church – Libreria Editrice Vaticana.

1. The Catechism of the Catholic Church – Libreria Editrice Vaticana.
2. Pope Francis, Evangelii Gaudium (2013), Laudato Si' (2015), and Fratelli Tutti (2020).
3. Joseph Ratzinger (Pope Benedict XVI), 'Introduction to Christianity' (1968), and various homilies.
4. Charles Taylor, 'A Secular Age' (2007).
5. Romano Guardini, 'The End of the Modern World' (1956).
6. Henri Nouwen, 'The Return of the Prodigal Son' (1992), 'The Way of the Heart' (1981).
7. Hans Urs von Balthasar, 'Prayer' (1955), 'The Glory of the Lord' (1961–1969).
8. Robert Cardinal Sarah, 'The Power of Silence' (2016).

9. T. S. Eliot, 'Four Quartets' (1943).
10. Wendell Berry, 'Standing by Words' (1983) and selected essays.
11. Official Vatican press releases and statements regarding the election of Pope Leo XIV (Robert Francis Prevost).
12. News commentary and profiles from Catholic News Service, National Catholic Reporter, Crux, and La Croix.
13. Historical material on the papacy from Eamon Duffy, 'Saints and Sinners: A History of the Popes' (1997).
14. Interviews, public addresses, and pastoral writings attributed to Cardinal Robert Francis Prevost.
15. General theological frameworks and ecclesial spirituality drawn from Ignatian and Benedictine traditions.

ABOUT THE AUTHOR

The author writes under a chosen name, not to hide, but to step back. This book is not offered as a personal reflection, but as a witness to something more lasting than biography. What matters is not who speaks, but what has been remembered, and whether it helps others remain close to what is true.

The author lives in silence more than online, in prayer more than public. This work was written slowly, with reverence, and without hurry.